JANUARY–A

VOLUME 14 / PART 1

◆▶ **The Bible Reading Fellowship**
O P E N I N G   T H E   B I B L E

Writers in this issue

Exodus 1–15 **Michael Tunnicliffe** is on the staff of the Northern Ordination Course. He is an ordained Methodist minister and has served in churches in Stoke-on-Trent and Birmingham.

1 Corinthians **Loveday Alexander** is Senior Lecturer in New Testament in the Department of Biblical Studies at Sheffield University. Her research interests lie in the writings of Luke: she is the author of *The Preface to Luke's Gospel*, Cambridge, 1993, and is currently working on a book on Acts. She has two grown-up children, and is an Anglican lay reader in her local parish church.

Jonah **Grace Emmerson** is an honorary lecturer in theology in the University of Birmingham. She has published work on various Old Testament subjects and lectures to church and other groups on biblical issues. Her involvement in parish work includes time spent in the Canadian Arctic. She is joint-editor of *Guidelines* and editor of BRF's companion to the prophetic books of the Old Testament, *Prophets and Poets*.

Daniel 1–7 **Michael Wadsworth** is Vicar of Haddenham and Wilburton, north of Cambridge, Rural Dean of Ely, and an Honorary Canon of Ely. He is also an Affiliated Lecturer in the Divinity Faculty of the University of Cambridge. He has been a lecturer in Religious Studies in the University of Sussex, Fellow and Chaplain of Sidney Sussex College, Cambridge, and a vicar of two Merseyside parishes, while holding the post of Lay Training officer in the Liverpool Diocese.

Mark 9–16 **Ian Wallis** is Rector of Houghton-le-Spring, County Durham. He was previously Chaplain of Sidney Sussex College, Cambridge. His major study *The Faith of Jesus Christ in Early Christian Traditions* was published by Cambridge University Press in 1995.

Isaiah 40–55 **John Eaton**, formerly Reader in Old Testament Studies in the University of Birmingham, has published work on many Old Testament subjects. His most recent book is *The Circle of Creation: Animals in the Light of the Bible*. He has a particular interest in spirituality and the arts.

THE BRF
Magazine

Shelagh Brown
1930–1997

It is with great sadness and a deep sense of personal loss that I must tell you that Shelagh Brown died in the early hours of Sunday 29 June 1997, just days before this edition of the *BRF Magazine* was due to go to press. She fell on the stairs at home, sustaining a head injury from which she never recovered, and died peacefully in the Intensive Care Ward of the John Radcliffe Hospital in Oxford.

Words cannot express adequately how much her loss means to us in BRF. Shelagh was not only a valued and highly respected colleague, but she was a great personal friend as well. Her contribution to BRF, as a Trustee from 1985 to 1991, as Editor of *New Daylight* from 1989, and as a Commissioning Editor of most of BRF's adult books from 1991, is incalculable. Her ministry extended worldwide through *New Daylight* and many of those who wrote to her talked of how they felt they almost knew her themselves, through her writing. Shelagh left no living relatives. Indeed her close friends, and BRF itself, were her family.

Shelagh was probably best known for her involvement with BRF, but this chapter in her life came after a wide-ranging career in both the secular world and the church. She had worked for a brief period as a secretary in the Press Office at Buckingham Palace, and over the years as personal assistant to Sir Edward Boyle, Professor Sir Norman Anderson, Sir Jock Logan, and Prebendary Dick Lucas. She was ordained deaconess in 1980, deacon in 1987, and priest at Pentecost in 1994. Among the churches where she served were St Mark's Reigate, Caterham Valley, and St Mary's Reigate.

Shelagh shared wholeheartedly the BRF aim of helping men and women of all ages to encounter the living God through regular Bible reading and prayer. Alongside her role as Editor of *New Daylight*, she was responsible for many of BRF's most successful books, most notably the annual Lent books. She was also an author in her own right, with several books published by BRF—*Feeding on God*, *Brushing up on Believing* and *Lights that Shine* (both with Bishop Gavin Reid), and *Lent for Busy People*. And she was one of the three General Editors of BRF's *The People's Bible Commentary Series*. It was Shelagh's idea that BRF should provide a series of commentaries to help lay people to work systematically through the whole Bible. At the time of her death the first five volumes had been published. The series will be completed as a tribute to her.

Shelagh was born in London, but grew up in Oxford. After living for many years in Reigate, Surrey, she moved back to Oxford in July 1995, a move which she always described as 'coming home'. The study in her home in Wolvercote, where she did much of her writing, overlooked Port Meadow, where she would walk as often as she could. She is buried in Wolvercote Cemetery, near her beloved Port Meadow and the river Thames.

A memorial fund has been established within BRF as a lasting tribute to Shelagh's outstanding contribution to the Kingdom of God. Among the projects for which this fund will be used will be The Shelagh Brown Memorial Prize to be awarded annually to a young writer who shows outstanding originality, creativity, and flair in communicating the Gospel. Donations to the fund should be sent to BRF. For more information please write to me at BRF.

Shelagh's notes on the Holy Spirit in 1 Corinthians, which appear at the end of the January 1998 issue of *New Daylight*, were her most recent writing project, completed only shortly before her death. How fitting that she should write in her note for 30 April: 'It will be through the empowering presence of God the Holy Spirit that we shall be raised up into the glory of our resurrection bodies.' She has indeed been raised up into that glory.

We at BRF are devastated by the sudden loss of Shelagh. We give grateful thanks for her life, but we deeply mourn her death. We ask you for your prayers in these difficult times.

Richard Fisher
Chief Executive

Richard Fisher writes

Happy New Year from all of us at BRF. I write at the end of the wettest June since 1987, and exactly a week after the safe arrival of our first child, Hannah. Although by the time you read this much of the news will be as much as six months old, it still provides an opportunity to give you news about BRF, its ministry, publications and people.

Staff News

By the time you read this, we will have said farewell to two members of the BRF staff team. Chris Samways, our Subscriptions Co-ordinator, leaves in July to move to Keynsham, where her husband John is to be the new Team Rector of the Keynsham Team Ministry. And Andrew Starkie, our Project Editor, leaves in August to move with his wife Rosalind and eighteen-month-old Thomas to Cambridge, to begin training for ordination at Ridley Hall. We will greatly miss both Chris and Andrew and wish them every blessing for the future.

Events

We have continued to enjoy the programme of events for the 75th anniversary year. It has been especially good to meet so many of our readers and supporters at the various occasions. We are planning more events as part of our regular annual programme (retreats, author events, special days, services, etc.) and if you would like information about these, please contract the BRF office.

New Publications

We are delighted to be able to publish jointly with Oxford University Press *The Way In New Testament*, which includes the complete New Testament text from the Anglicised *New Revised Standard Version* along with an Introduction and over fifty articles by David Winter. You can read more about *The Way In New Testament* on page 26. The new Lent book for 1998 is *Reflecting the Glory* by bestselling author and New Testament expert Tom Wright (see page 22 for an extract), and we have published *The Easter Treasure Hunt* for children aged 5-8.

Livewires

We have been very pleased with the response we have had to the *Livewires* series. They are very different from the old *First Light* notes, but we have had very positive comments from former *First Light* readers who have given the new material a try. Six *Livewires* volumes are now available, each a complete adventure in their own right, but part of a highly collectable ongoing series. The *Livewires* books are aimed primarily at the individual child to read themselves, and are ideal for Parents, Grandparents and Godparents who want their children to be able to learn about the people, the places and events of the Bible in an imaginative and accessible way. We shall shortly be publishing a teacher's guide which will provide all you need to use material from the first six volumes in a class or group setting.

Disciple

The *Disciple* course continues to gather momentum within churches in the UK. My own church is about to begin its second *Disciple* group, and more and more churches are enrolling in the programme. There will be a number of leader training events throughout 1998, so if you would like details, please send an A4 38p s.a.e marked 'Disciple' in the top left hand corner to the BRF in Oxford.

Church Magazines

Most churches have a weekly or monthly magazine. During the past year we have received a growing number of requests for information about BRF and its publications from those who would like to include this in their church magazine—perhaps in the lead up to Bible Sunday, or in order to raise the profile of Bible reading in the church, or because they want to keep others in touch with what BRF can offer in terms of resources. If you yourself are the editor of your church magazine, or you think that the editor might like to receive information of this kind from BRF on a regular basis, why not write and let us know so we can put you on our mailing list?

And finally

As we look forward to 1998, and all the challenges and opportunities that it will bring, we hope and pray that you will know God's presence and his blessings throughout the year ahead.

On Loving God

John Fenton

Somebody (and I forget who it was) has pointed out that had we not been *commanded* to love God, we should never have thought of it for ourselves as something we should try to do.

It would not have been difficult for us to think that we should fear God, keep his laws, and avoid offending him in any way. We might also have thought of praising him, thanking him, even worshipping and adoring him. But *loving* God would not be what anyone would think of, on their own. It had to come to us as a commandment. We could not have made it up for ourselves.

The reason why this is so is that we think of love as only possible between people of more or less equal status, particularly if it is to be love with all our heart, all our soul, all our mind and all our strength. Though we might say that we love the Queen Mother on the one hand, or the cat and the dog on the other, in none of these cases is love remotely like what it can be when it is between husbands and wives, brothers and sisters, parents and children, friends and colleagues, men and women. Yet what we are commanded to do is to love God, who is even less like us than any other human being or any animal or place, or anything else

that might be the object of our love. He is the one and only creator of everything that is, and all the rest of us are creatures. Can we really love what is totally different from us? It is so unexpected, and seems so improbable, it had to be given as a commandment.

Moreover the commandment to love God is said to be the first of all the commandments, both in Judaism and in Christianity. Jesus says so in Mark (12:28–34) and the scribe agrees with him. In Luke (10:25–28) it is the lawyer who says it, and Jesus agrees with the lawyer. In both Gospels what is being quoted is Deuteronomy (6:5): You must love the Lord your God with all your heart and with all your soul and with all your strength.

It is an indication of how much Christianity has changed, from what it was at certain times in the past, that it is very unlikely that anyone today, when asked the question, 'What is it that Christians (or Jews, for that matter, I suppose) believe that they should try to do?', would reply, 'The first commandment,' which is sometimes also called the greatest commandment (Matthew 22:38), 'is to love God.' We would be far more likely to say that our chief concern was to care for other people, avoid evil in all its forms and everything else that comes within the coverage of the second commandment, 'Love your neighbour as yourself', which, like the first, is also a quotation from the Hebrew scriptures (Leviticus 19:18).

Attempts have been made at various times to reduce the two commandments to one. The writer of The First Letter of John imagines someone saying 'I love God', while at the same time hating his fellow-Christian. He says that such a claim is a lie: not to love a fellow-Christian renders one incapable of loving God (4:20). We cannot opt out of the second commandment by supposedly obeying the first. Nor, on the other hand, is it possible to think that observance of the second is a way of satisfying the first: as though by loving our neighbour we had no further need to think about God and what we owe to him. The two-foldness of the commandments is made explicit in the Gospels. Although Jesus is asked which is the first, he replies with two, the first and the second, and he refers to them in the plural:

... there is an obvious connection between loving and giving...

'No other commandment is greater than these' (Mark 12:28–31).

What is to be said, then, if the question is asked, 'How do I love God?' 'What do I do to express love for the one who is not seen?'

For a start, there is an obvious connection between loving and giving, and this understanding of what the Catechism calls our duty towards God is the basis of the list of religious good works in the Sermon on the Mount: alms-giving, prayer and fasting. Sometimes this section of the Sermon is presented as though alms-giving, prayer and fasting were only practised among the hypocrites, not by the disciples of Jesus. But this is not what is said. What is said is, 'When you give alms'; 'when you pray'; 'when you fast'. In each case, something is being given away: money, time and physical enjoyment. Here are three ways of expressing love for God.

Secondly, approving of God and his ways is another aspect of loving him. It would be inconsistent to love God and loathe the world that he has made and for which, ultimately, he is entirely responsible, since there is no other God apart from him. The commandment to love him involves us in an attitude of acceptance of the world as it is, even though in some respects this must seem nearly impossible, for example when one thinks of disease, congenital defects, cruelty and the apparent pointlessness of life for so many. Even so, one could not love the creator if one hated his creation, or despised it, or did not care about it at all.

Thirdly, it would not be possible to love God if you had doubts about his attitude to you. You can only love, in the sense of the first commandment, somebody whom you can trust. If we were to find ourselves constantly wondering whether we might eventually be condemned by him for all the mistakes we had made, and rightly condemned, because we really had made these mistakes and deserved condemnation, it would not be possible to love God. That we are commanded to love him tells us all that we need to know about his attitude to us:

> *It would not be possible to love God if you had doubts about his attitude to you*

that he loves what he has made, and that he has reconciled us to himself, and that he cares for what he sustains and will not let it fall from his hands.

It may be that our sense of God and of our duty towards him—that is, of the first and greatest commandment—is so weak and fragile that we need to read books by the older authors, who excelled us so notably in this matter. Some of the books I have in mind are: Saint Augustine's *Confessions*; Thomas à Kempis' *The Imitation of Christ*; Richard Rolle's *The Fire of Love*; *The Cloud of Unknowing*; Walter Hilton's *The Ladder of Perfection*; and Julian of Norwich's *Revelations of Divine Love*. These, and other books that can help us in this way, are all published in versions that are easy to read, in Penguin Classics.

John Fenton *is the author of* The Matthew Passion, *and of* Galatians *in the* People's Bible Commentary *Series. Both are published by BRF and are available from your local Christian bookshop or, in case of difficulty, direct from BRF. For details, see order form, page 159.*

Draw near with faith

Joy Tetley

The congregation looked as if they really did not want to be there. Discouragement was written all over their faces. The atmosphere was depressed, and there was a distinct edge of fear.

In years gone by things had been very different. God had seemed very real to them *then*. All kinds of exciting things had happened—signs and wonders and mighty works. There had been some very hard times, too—times when they had suffered much, just for being Christian. But their faith had carried them through, and their sense of joy in the Lord had never left them, even in those testing times.

But now, now that joy seemed a remote dream—and their faith was all but gone. Danger seemed the primary reality. As followers of Jesus, hostility against them was becoming intense. This time, they could hardly bear it. And God seemed to be doing nothing. No signs and wonders now. No great acts of deliverance. Nothing.

What was the point of the gospel, then, if God did not come to their help when he was most needed? What was the point of trusting in Jesus, if life got harder rather than easier? What was the point of meeting together for worship, when it did nothing for them, except lay them more open to abuse and persecution? Wouldn't it be safer to give up any allegiance to Jesus?

Perhaps their Christian commitment had all been a dreadful mistake anyway. Perhaps it might even be that God was punishing them for not staying true to the Jewish faith in which they had been nurtured. Perhaps *that* was why he was hiding his face.

Disheartened, confused, afraid, ready to give up, this congregation has met together to hear an urgent communication from someone who knew them well; someone who had authority over them but who, for some reason, could not be with them in person. He has sent them a sermon, a sermon born out of his passionate concern for their deepest welfare; his passionate concern at this critical time to keep them on the way of Christ, on the way of Jesus.

That sermon we find in the New Testament, described as the Epistle

11

to the Hebrews. Its call to persevering faith, even in the most dire of circumstances, speaks powerfully across the centuries. It speaks not of an impossible ideal, but of a faithful God, who stays with the needy through the bleakest of experiences and, in the strongest possible sense, takes their distress to his heart. So all can draw near with faith because they have a God whose commitment to them is absolute—at all times and in all places.

That's a claim that needs exploring. So let's explore by looking at some extracts from this amazing sermon, a sermon, incidentally, in which head and heart are brought very tellingly together. We focus first on one of the key passages of the whole work— Hebrews 4:12–16. [NB Joy Tetley will deal with the second paragraph of this key passage in the next issue of *New Daylight*.]

Indeed, the word of God is living and active, sharper than any two-edged sword, piercing until it divides soul from spirit, joints from marrow; it is able to judge the thoughts and intentions of the heart. And before him no creature is hidden, but all are naked and laid bare to the eyes of the one to whom we must render an account.

Since then, we have a great high priest who has passed through the heavens, Jesus, the Son of God, let us hold fast to our confession. For we do not have a high priest who is unable to sympathise with our weaknesses, but we have one who in every respect has been tested as we are, yet without sin. Let us therefore approach the throne of grace with boldness, so that we may receive mercy and find grace to help in time of need. (NRSV)

Absolutely nothing can be hidden from the one to whom we have to give an account

The opening sentences of that passage are a fearsome reminder that absolutely nothing can be hidden from the one to whom we have to give an account. The language is extreme; it's graphic, it's chilling. Here is total vulnerability. The story of Adam and Eve's failure in Eden is very much implicit at this point, and the preacher of Hebrews means his hearers to take its implications very seriously indeed. After the disobedience which reveals their nakedness, Adam and Eve try to hide from God, but they are further exposed, both outwardly and inwardly, by God's voice, God's penetrating words: 'Where are you?' So it is with you, says the preacher. No excuses will do. No shifting of blame. No disowning of personal responsibility. Your condition is utterly transparent to God. No amount of pretending or 'cover-up' can change that reality.

Well, to a struggling and disheartened congregation, that message does not, at first hearing, seem full of hope. Yet the preacher wants to lift these people out of despair, not push them further into it. And he's perceptive enough to realize that the turning point is not likely to come until those he calls elsewhere his 'beloved ones' fully acknowledge the reality of their state in every area of life. Fundamental honesty opens up new possibilities.

And the truth about themselves has to be brought face to face with the truth about God. The kind of God before whom they are exposed, before whom they are totally vulnerable, is of critical significance. Will this God come to destroy? The congregation already has a clue in the Genesis creation narrative the preacher has alluded to. Though Adam and Eve had to bear responsibility for their failure, God nonetheless continued to care for and about them. The full truth revealed in Jesus, insists the preacher, is even more encouraging. Though, before God, these discouraged folk are stripped of all pretence, with their imperfections, their weaknesses, laid bare, they have nothing to fear. Despite their parlous state, they can approach God's presence, not in terror but in boldness (and the Greek word that's used there, *parresia* is a very interesting one. It means boldness, confidence, honesty, total frankness, freedom of speech). It's the very opposite of terrified grovelling.

As with that congregation, so with us. We can draw near to the throne of grace, with that same boldness. Liberated from the need to put on an act, we can be ourselves with God. We can be assured of receiving mercy—not condemnation—mercy, and finding grace to help in our time of need. We can go to God and tell how it is, however grim that might be. We don't have to pretend. What a relief! (What a relief! We don't have to pretend with God.)

The reason we can be so utterly confident lies in the nature of God. If we are laid bare before God, claims the preacher, God lays himself bare before us. Here is a God who, rather than deploring and punishing our condition, enters into it, feeling in Jesus the full force of temptation and human frailty. God identifies with us. God draws near to where we are—at tremendous cost to himself. God knows; God understands; God cares. Out of that knowing God can bring deep encouragement and mighty help.

> *God draws near to where we are—at tremendous cost to himself.*

13

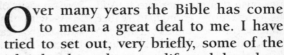

My debt to the Bible

Donald Coggan

Over many years the Bible has come to mean a great deal to me. I have tried to set out, very briefly, some of the enrichments which it has brought to my life and thought.

When you find a treasure it is a good idea to share it with others. If 'a sorrow shared is a sorrow halved', it's equally true that a treasure shared is a treasure multiplied. Let me do this under five headings.

1. The Bible has given me a love of literature.

I can remember the day when I was first given a copy of the Greek New Testament. Though New Testament Greek is not of the best classical style, but is, rather, the Greek of the market-place and of the fireside, it yet retains much of the fluidity and exactitude of expression which we associate with that lovely language. When, as a boy at school, I learned the elements of Hebrew, and later pursued those studies at Cambridge and taught the language at Manchester University, I came into touch with a language rougher, tougher, more abrasive than Greek, but one which was well adapted to convey the utterances of prophets and seers.

After a while, the Bible in English continued to make its mark upon me. As a boy, I went to the school where Lancelot Andrewes had studied three and a half centuries before, and I came in time to learn how great his contribution had been to the making of that superb work of English literature, the so-called Authorized Version of 1611. Indeed, Sir Arthur Bryant has called it 'the supreme literary legacy of the Tudor age'. Behind the figure of the great bishop, I came to picture the towering personality of William Tyndale, some 90 per cent of whose translation is incorporated in the Authorized Version. I learned to appreciate the power of monosyllabic English—'thus will I bless thee while I live; I will lift up my hands in thy name'.

The study of language is a training in exactitude of thought and expression and in the appreciation of literary beauty. In the study of the Bible, whether in English or in its original languages, a great variety of riches spreads itself before the reader—prose and verse, history and parable, love song and battle story, letters and theses, proverbs and apocalypse. It is a rich inheritance.

2. The Bible has given me a love of history.

Across the pages of the Bible the nations pass, one after another in strange procession—Egypt and Babylon, Persia and Greece, Rome... The potentates of time rise and flourish, wax and wane—the Pharaohs here, Cyrus ('Yahweh's anointed'!) and Nebuchadnezzar there; Alexander the Great dying aged thirty-three; the Caesars ruling with rough justice and at times with megalomaniac brutality.

And there in their midst is little Israel, pawn of the nations, the Belgium of the ancient world, the darling of the Lord.

We cannot watch this historical drama and fail to take history seriously. Our sights are lifted. We assent to Bishop Lesslie Newbigin's dictum: 'The object of God's reign is human (and cosmic) history as a whole'; and to Max Warren's assertion: 'Isolating the Church from history is another way of being anti-Christ.' No one can read the Bible with the seriousness it deserves without being brought face to face with a people who viewed history as the arena in which God was performing his mighty deeds and working out his salvation.

3. The Bible has stretched my mind with great concepts.

Often beyond the full grasp of human comprehension, great and basic ideas are wrestled with in these pages—election and predestination, sin and salvation, life and death, heaven and hell, Church and world, God, Christ, Holy Spirit... Here are subjects which have occupied the minds of great people, men and women not content to live life on the animal level of satisfaction of temporal desires, but desirous of stretching mind and spirit almost to breaking-point if truth can thereby be found.

Here in the Bible are priests, prophets, seers, evangelists, men of the desert who went out into silence that they might come back with a word, a word which itself was a fire burning in their bones, a burden from which they could only find release by a costly uttering of it. Here are men and women who know that ideas and ideals matter, mould, make men and women and nations.

No one who wrestles with the immensities of the biblical revelation can be content with trivialities, nor can they succumb to unintelligent bibliolatry. Readers of the Bible find themselves enlarged as they welcome truth from all quarters and exercise intellectual honesty in handling it.

4. The Bible has introduced me to great people.

Here I meet **Abraham**, striding out, at the call of God, from the comforts and high civilization of Ur, to found a nation destined to be the agent of God's redemptive purpose—a giant of faith;

Moses, destined to bring that people up to the border of the land of their possession, learning through hard experience how great he was (the son of Pharaoh's daughter), how small he was (tending his father-in-law's flock) and, eventually, how great God was in taking him up into his purposes;

Job, of all men the most impatient, crying out about the blatant injustices of God's world, buffeted as he himself was by an unbelieving wife and an impossible trio of pseudo-comforters;

Isaiah, brought up in court circles, watching the fall of his idol monarch, Uzziah, coming face to face with a greater King, called to go out and proclaim a message of divine judgment;

Jeremiah, young and diffident, crying out against a God who had, so he said in his bitterest moment, deceived him, and yet unable to keep silent because God's word was like a fire in his bones and he could not contain it;

Amos, no prophet nor a prophet's son, but a herdsman to whom the Lord's call came with undeniable power;

Hosea, whose marital tragedy became the instrument of a gospel because, through it, he saw into the broken heart of God;

Mary, the village girl who dared to say: 'Behold the handmaid of the Lord; be it unto me according to thy will', and taught her son to pray that prayer, too;

Peter, the master of insight, the man of foolish speech, coward and truant, witness and apostle, evangelist and martyr;

John, the beloved, young, mystic, literary musician who from a synoptic idea could compose a fugue, the man whose symbol is, so rightly, an eagle, for it is said that that bird soars nearer to the sun than any other;

Paul, convert, traveller, correspondent, pastor, apostle, martyr, a man in Christ, debtor to Jews and Gentiles and, above all, to Christ, slave of Jesus, churchman;

We meet them all, and many besides in the pages of the Bible. We get to know them over the years, and in the knowing find ourselves uplifted.

5. The Bible has conveyed Christ to me.

Here the sacramental principle is at work. In the Holy Communion the Holy Spirit takes ordinary bread and wine, the stuff of life which we handle every day, and by means of these ordinary things conveys the life and vivacity of Christ to his people in the Church. Similarly, when a group of disciples or an individual humbly takes this book written by ordinary people, with the marks of time and the difficulties caused by transmisison evidently upon it, the Holy Spirit gets to work and conveys Christ through it to the mind and heart and conscience of the reader. He effects an introduction between the sincere and honest seeker and him who is the central figure of the book. Martin Luther was right when he spoke of the Bible as the cradle which bears

Christ to us; we do not worship the Bible; we are not bibliolators; but we worship and adore the Christ whom we see in its pages.

As we saw under the previous section, the Bible is, from one point of view, a portrait gallery—rulers, priests, prophets, saints, prostitutes, fishermen, tax-gatherers, scholars, prisoners, refugees, warriors, traitors, martyrs, all are there. But one portrait stands out from all the rest in such a way as to make nonsense of the gallery without it. It is the portrait of Jesus Christ, Son of God and Son of Man.

As he looks out at us from the pages of the Bible, somehow he ceases to be a figure of the historic past, and presents himself to us as a living person in the present. He may look at us with rebuke, as he once did to Philip ('Have I been so long with you, Philip, and still you have not come to know me?'); or with disappointment, as he did to Peter when he had denied him; or with imperious invitation, as he did to the young quartet by the lake ('Come, follow me'); or with penetrating question, as he did to Saul of Tarsus ('Why are you persecuting me?'). But if, as he looks at us, we return the look in adoration and committal, in that exchange we enter into life abundant.

The Bible has then fulfilled its main function.

To many people, the Bible is a closed book. They cannot be altogether blamed for this. They may be reading it in an ancient version, all cluttered up with cross-references. There are plenty of translations in modern English, and they help a great deal. People need a guide. There are plenty to hand.

Often there are difficulties because people do not know where to begin. They start at Genesis and soon find themselves in a world of ideas wholly foreign to them. They would do better to begin with one of the four Gospels, which tell of the life and teaching, the death and resurrection of Jesus Christ, for example the Gospel of St Luke. Then they could go on to watch the young lively Church in action (The Acts of the Apostles), and thence to the letters which give a slant of the writers on the great events which had recently happened in the Holy Land and which were to shake the world.

When they have done that, they may feel the need to understand something of the background against which these writings came down to us, the scriptures which Jesus himself read and pondered, and so they will begin to have a look at the Old Testament. Here it might be the course of wisdom to begin with some of the writings of the Prophets—for they were towering figures who had words of immense importance for the men and women of their day. They have a timeless quality about them.

A visit to Barbados

Rosemary Green

The Anglican church in Barbados came in with the British colonisers 250 years ago. It was disestablished in 1969, a few years after the nation got its independence, but it is still widely regarded as the 'proper' church to belong to among this warm and churchgoing people.

Driving round with the Bishop it was remarkable to see how many people greeted him as the car passed! Congregations remain large, but there is much nominalism, and a considerable falling off of men and of young people; the average congregation is probably 90 per cent women, the majority of them over sixty. The Church is strongly Anglo-Catholic in its externals, having been greatly influenced by the Mirfield monks in the last century, and nearly all the clergy of the Province of the West Indies are trained under the same influences at Codrington College (the oldest theological college in the Western hemisphere). There is little atheism in the country, but at the same time the society is increasingly secular (with much of the time on

> *There is little atheism in the country, but at the same time the society is increasingly secular*

TV filled with American soaps) and faces the same problems of drugs and postmodernism as the rest of the Western world does.

Against this background it is remarkable that the Bible Reading Fellowship has a huge membership. About 1665 copies of the notes are distributed by Mrs Madeleine Smith, who works indefatigably for the BRF. This is about 1/55 of the total world-wide membership of the BRF— amazing when we think of the tiny size of the island (about 160 square miles) with its population of 265,000 people. Few of the parishes have any small Bible study groups, but it is the BRF that has spawned some of the groups that do exist.

My husband and I were in Barbados for a two-week diocesan

mission. We were amused when the Bishop introduced us at a press conference on the first day. 'We have known Michael Green through his books' (holding up a copy of one of his books) 'and we have known Rosemary Green through the Bible Reading Fellowship' (showing a well worn copy of the current *New Daylight*) 'but we had not connected the two!'

One of the events during the fortnight was a service to celebrate the BRF's 75th Anniversary. It was modelled on the one which was held in Westminster Abbey in January 1997 and included singing Timothy Dudley-Smith's hymns written for that occasion. At the start of my sermon I asked if anyone who had been a BRF member for more than 20 years would stand up. Several people stood. "Please stay standing if you have belonged for 30 years… 40 years… 50 years." There were still some on their feet! In fact as the congregation left one lady told me that she was too shy to stand up— but she had been reading BRF notes since 1932 (when BRF was only 10 years old, and limited in its size and distribution). Can anyone beat that?

Free range hens that scratch for their own food give tastier eggs

In my sermon I spoke of the privilege of writing notes that seek to bring the Bible to life for readers all over the world. At the same time I suggested that they should not rely on the writers' comments. It is the free range hens that scratch for their own food that give tastier eggs than the chickens in the factory farm that need to make no effort to reach their pre-pared food as it goes past on the conveyor belt; that is as true in Barbados as it is elsewhere! So I encouraged them to read the passage, then do their own thinking, before turning to the notes.

So greetings to BRF members all over the world—and especially to my new friends in Barbados!

Bible story
Marcus Maxwell

In some distant jungle, a new tribe is contacted for the first time. Anthropologists go to study it. How do they go about the task? One of the most important ways is to listen to the stories that are told by the tribe. Sat round the campfire at night, tales are told of the origin of this people, of its history and its gods, of its adventures, triumphs and disasters.

By listening to these stories, the children learn what it is to be a member of the tribe. They learn the tribe's understanding of right and wrong, what to hope for, what to aim for, and how to measure success and failure. The adults gain fresh encouragement for their daily work, and re-affirm their pride in belonging.

The stories are now going to change. A new tale will be told, of the strange newcomers who can do such wonderful things, and yet are the slaves of the devices they wear on their wrists. The new story will contradict some of the earlier ones, telling of a world that is wider and more varied than that of the old story-tellers. The basic story and outlook of the tribe will change forever.

Our own tribe behaves in exactly the same way. We understand the world, ourselves, and our place in the world, by telling stories. It's clear that we use stories to teach our children. Before they arrive in school, much of our children's view of the world is shaped by tales told by their parents, their friends and the Walt Disney Corporation.

Throughout our lives, we go on telling stories, and fitting new items of understanding and belief into those stories. If that sounds a bit far-fetched, let me give you an example. In last year's British general election, a lot of noise was made about Europe, and Britain's role in it. On the surface, argument raged around terms such as 'sovereignty', 'self-determination', 'single currency', 'federalism' and what have you. What was actually going on was the telling of two stories, both fairly familiar, but in competition with each other.

There was the tale of the brave island nation, which throughout its early history had been invaded by Europeans, from the Romans to the Normans. As the nation developed (becoming a bastion of truth, freedom and democracy) it had fought off later European threats, most notably defeating Napoleon, Kaiser Wilhelm and Hitler. It had from time to time made righteous forays into Europe (in the cause of truth, freedom and democracy) but always had retained its free and courageous spirit. Now a new threat looms. The spiritual descendants of Napoleon and the Kaiser are poised to invade, using the weapons of a single currency, a borderless Europe and the

European Court of Human Rights. True to our history, we must resist as we resisted the Spanish Armada.

The second story told of a Brave Britain which had long stood aloof from the turmoil and disaster of European history. Now, after centuries of war and confusion, a new dawn is breaking over Europe, and a time of unity and prosperity lies ahead. Britain, with its great heritage of truth, freedom and democracy (and its dire economic need) has an important role to play. Europe needs us, and we need it. Together, we can form a brave new world.

The question to be decided is which story best fits the facts. Which one describes reality most fully and satisfyingly? In short, which one has the best claim to be true?

You may well say that you have never heard anyone tell either of those stories out loud. Perhaps not. Yet we still recognise them, don't we? That's the point about our most important and basic stories. They are rarely told as simple little tales, yet they are told bit by bit in a thousand assumptions and attitudes which we take for granted day by day.

Most importantly, these stories change, as new ones are told, which challenge and undermine the old ones, like the tale of the white people who came to the jungle folk and changed the old narrative.

What is the most basic story that people tell today? I think it goes something like this. The universe exists, who knows why? Out of it, by pure fluke, came life. By a vast series of coincidences and chance events, some of that life became intelligent, self-aware people who ask questions. They wonder what it is all about, where it is going, and what they are worth. There are no true answers, and they are doomed to disappointment. In the end they will disappear, having been around for a while, and invented all sorts of diversions to try to lend meaning to a pointless world. Some time later, the universe will wind down, either to disappear in silence or begin the whole process over again.

Few tell the story out loud, but it underlies contemporary life. There is little wonder, then, if everything from self-respect to morality is up for grabs. In the end, all is pointless.

Christians, though, tell another story, of a universe which exists because God created it. It has a purpose, to bring forth creatures which are intelligent, self-aware and responsible. Creatures which have the capacity to know God, to sin and fall away from him. Into this world of broken dreams, comes God himself to call us back home, to share our pain and bear our failure. The best that the universe has produced will not be lost for ever, but preserved in an eternal relationship with its creator.

It is this story which we find in the Bible, and retell as Christians, by the way we live, speak and pray. It is a story which still has power to change lives. It is the story which will be told for all eternity, because it is God's story.

Reflecting the Glory

an extract from BRF's 1998 Lent book by Tom Wright

It is at the heart of Christianity that the one we call 'God' is known in Jesus. Christians find that very difficult to take on board, because we know the stories of Jesus both too well and not well enough. 'Oh yes, I know this one,' we think, and so we turn the parable of the prodigal son simply into a lesson about the love of God.

Then we generalize it and say, 'Yes, of course God loves us'—without realizing the peculiar dynamic, the intensity and the drama which is going on in the parable. So we constantly need to go back and remind ourselves who Jesus actually was and what he was actually like and what the particular emphases of his parables actually were.

One of the reasons why we fight shy of doing that is that the more we make Jesus a believable first-century Jew the harder it often is for us to see what this Jesus has to say to *us*—either about God or about ourselves and our lives. We aren't first-century Jews. We aren't being invaded by the Roman army. We aren't asking questions about paying tribute to Caesar. We haven't got those problems. So what we often do is to reduce the message of Jesus. We turn it into a timeless, abstract statement of generalized truths which are, frankly, boring. Then we imagine that we have this thing called 'truth' in our pocket—and those of us who are theologians and teachers produce it and shove it down people's throats.

Whereas the truth about God in Jesus is not that sort of thing. Truth is more like health. Doctors don't keep 'health' in their pocket, so that all they have to do is to put in a hand and take it out and give it to people. Doctors can do things which create the conditions for health and which reduce the possibilities of un-health. But ultimately health is a strange, mysterious thing which is part of God's gift of life. So it is with truth.

The truth as it is in Jesus is personal truth. So that not only are we summoned as Christians to *see* God in Jesus, but also to *know* God in Jesus. And, ultimately, to *love* God in Jesus. You can't love an abstraction. You can't even love the idea of love. You can love a piece of music—but the deepest, richest meaning of love must be personal love. You can only really love a person. And when we love God in Jesus, in response to God's love for us, then we discover that that love, that personality, that personal love is given *to* us in order that it may be given *through* us.

The realization of this dynamic truth was the reason why Christians from the very beginning spoke of the Holy Spirit. Because the Spirit is the one who enables us to know that we are loved by God and also to love Jesus. The Spirit actually is the presence of Jesus in us, enabling us to love one another and to shine the light of God's love into the world. This is that great transition, that great turning of the corner, which means that the more we find out about Jesus (and particularly his death and resurrection, precisely because it is historically grounded) then the more we are energized by the Spirit to be Christ for the world.

For me the great turning point of all this is in John chapter 20, where Jesus breathes on his disciples and says to them, 'Receive the Holy Spirit. As the Father sent me, so I send you.' And suddenly we see the whole vista of all that God did in Jesus, with his healings and his rejections and his parables, and the extraordinary celebration and the extraordinary agony. And we discover that that is not only what we can truly say about *Jesus*, but it is now what *we* are called to do and be in the power of the Spirit for the world. Then we realize that this is the vocation of the Christian—to take up our cross and be Jesus for the world, with the celebration and the sorrow all written into that equation. There is the most remarkable joy, and the most remarkable sorrow.

So, in the light of all of that, what we are doing in this particular Lent is beginning with one of the most deeply personal and profoundly felt passages in all of the New Testament, with Paul having got to the end of his tether. And not only to the end of his tether but beyond it. Early in 2 Corinthians he says that 'I felt utterly crushed, so that I despaired of life itself.' Part of what was crushing him was the fact that the Corinthian Church, with whom he had lived and worked for quite a long time, was quite casually rejecting him. And in this passage, which we shall be looking at for the first two weeks or so of Lent, he is writing to tell them that they have got things totally wrong. That the pain he has suffered, and the puzzles and the failings and the difficulties because of which they are rejecting him (since what they want is for him to be some sort of super Apostle), are actually the very things which are the mark of an Apostle. They aren't things which mean he isn't much of an Apostle. When you look at me, he is saying to them, you can see what it means to be bearing about in the body the dying of Jesus, as well as the life of Jesus. The whole middle section of 2 Corinthians (3:1—6:13) is all about what it means to have the love and faithfulness of God in Jesus worked out, by the Spirit, in Christian ministry and in apostolic living.

After that, we take several other passages both from Paul and from the first letter of Peter, and then look at Revelation. And in them we see that same picture taken and worked out almost kaleidoscopically through different writers. Each one explores what it means to have the suffering and the glory of Christ incarnated into them by the Spirit, so that they are then able to be the people of God for the world.

With that as a transition, we take a deep breath and launch into the Gospel of John, which will take us up to Holy Saturday. To begin with we follow through the theme of who Jesus is in the purpose of God. He is the one in whom the glory of God is revealed, and he is constantly challenging people both to see God's glory in him and then to become themselves the bearers and the vessels of God's glory. Throughout the first twelve chapters of John's Gospel even the disciples don't understand what's going on, let alone the onlookers. Again, the challenge is constantly going out: to see God's glory in Jesus, and then to be God's glory for the world.

Then from Passion Sunday and through Palm Sunday and Holy Week to Holy Saturday we shall be looking at the so-called farewell discourses, John 13 to 17. We shall see Jesus gathering together the threads of all that he has done. We shall hear him saying to his followers, 'Listen, this is what has been going on in my work, and now this is how it is going to be for you.' He is saying it to the eleven, to his close followers. (Judas had left them after the foot-washing.)

Then that message is gathered together into one in that extraordinary prayer in John 17, which is known as the great high priestly prayer of Jesus—the prayer which Jesus prayed on behalf of Christians in the world. He prays in it for the Church and for the widening company of all those who will come to believe in him through what the Eleven will do. So in keeping the cycle of Lent we shall go through the last three days: Maundy Thursday, where Jesus is actually praying that prayer but also living it in the last supper; Good Friday, where he is acting as the great high priest, and doing that to which the prayer is pointing; and then Holy Saturday, reflecting on the stillness, the extraordinary long breath before Easter Day—reflecting on Jesus the great high priest having gone to the lowest point of human experience, and gone into the valley of the shadow of death on behalf of his people.

Then from Easter Sunday, for the first seven days of Easter, we shall look at one of the most spectacular chapters of the New Testament—1 Corinthians 15. This was the first written exposition of resurrection and all that it means. In a great, sustained argument Paul explains to the Corinthians, point by point, what actually happened, what it all means and, particularly, where they belong on this extraordinary new map that God has just drawn, the map of Easter life.

What we shall be doing throughout this Lent is looking at the dying and rising of Jesus, both as the revelation once for all of the glory of God, and as the blueprint, the pattern, the energy and the vocation which is now given to God's people through his Spirit.

Tom Wright is Dean of Lichfield. A leading New Testament scholar, he has written many books at both a popular and academic level. His most recent books include *The Original Jesus* and *What Saint Paul Really Said* (both Lion Publishing).

Reflecting the Glory is available from your local Christian bookshop or, in case of difficulty, direct from BRF. See order form, page 159.

The Way In New Testament

with Introduction & articles by David Winter

The *Way In New Testament* provides a new introductory level guide to the teaching of the New Testament. It brings together the authoritative and increasingly popular *New Revised Standard Version* of the Bible in its Anglicised format, with more than fifty articles from one of today's finest communicators of the Christian faith. The result is a New Testament that uses the finest translation and allows the reader to explore the major doctrinal themes of the New Testament in a simple, yet surprisingly detailed way. All the major subjects are covered, using non-technical language that assumes limited prior knowledge. *The Way in New Testament* is ideal as a teaching resource for new Christians, but will offer stimulating new thoughts to readers of every age and tradition.

The Rt Revd James Jones, Bishop of Hull, writes commending *The Way In New Testament*:

'David Winter is an outstanding apologist. He brings his talent to the vitally important task of enabling people to read and understand the Bible. Without a knowledge of the Scriptures the Millennium is a mystery for it is only in these pages that we find an authoritative account of Jesus Christ. David Winter, through his introduction and notes, unpacks with clarity and originality the relevance of the Christian faith to a new generation who have yet to encounter its liberating and transforming power.'

The Way In New Testament is a joint publication with Oxford University Press. BRF is publishing the paperback and OUP the hardback edition.

David Winter is well known to BRF readers and supporters. Former head of religious broadcasting at the BBC and a regular presenter on Radio Four's 'Thought for the Day', he is the author of numerous books on many aspects of the Christian faith. These include *Forty Days with the Messiah, What's in a Word?*, *Mark for Starters* and *Come On In*, all published by BRF. David has been a regular contributor to *New Daylight* for a number of years, and is one of the General Editors of BRF's *People's Bible Commentary Series*.

The following extract is his Introduction to *The Way In New Testament*.

Introduction

There is a great interest today in the ideas and teaching of Jesus, with many books and television programmes purporting to reveal hitherto unknown 'facts' about him. Yet there is considerable ignorance, or at least confusion, about the actual content of the New Testament, despite the fact that centuries of painstaking research and investigation have shown it to be the most reliable source of information about him. It seems likely that many modern people pick up the New Testament, but when they start to read it they find its ideas and language unfamiliar and strange. This, after all, is not a world they can instantly recognize. Almost at once they are confronted by ideas that are foreign to them—angels, ancient prophecies, astrologers, evil spirits. Baffled, they give up the attempt.

Not only that, but words which they *do* recognize seem to be used in rather different ways. Modern people are familiar with covenants, justification, and even redemption—but not in the way the New Testament understands them! Even words like 'hope' or 'temptation' seem to have undergone a subtle change of meaning.

So the present-day reader needs some help when he or she turns to the New Testament, not so much because it is difficult—after all, it has a marvellously strong story to tell—but because it is different. This edition of the New Testament sets out to provide that help.

It does it through fifty-three explanatory articles, which pick up some of the major ideas and themes of the New Testament and 'unpack' them for the modern reader. These articles occur throughout the book, usually alongside a reference in the biblical text to the idea or theme under discussion. But there is also an alphabetical list of the topics covered, and the reader can always refer to this if help is needed with a particular word or idea, wherever it crops up.

The intention is to present this information in non-technical language, and without assuming any prior knowledge of the Bible on the part of the reader. But it will still require a willingness on his or her part to try to look at things through the eyes of the culture in which the New Testament books were written. It was an age of story, vision, and imagination, an age of deep and sometimes narrow religious commitment, an age when poverty, sickness, and death haunted every life and shaded every experience. Of course, in many ways the people who wrote the New Testament books, and the people for whom they wrote them, are remarkably like us, but in other important ways they were very different, and it is part of the excitement of reading these documents to enjoy the difference.

The New Testament has a 'hero', of course—Jesus of Nazareth. And it has a plot: the unfolding of God's plan to bring people back to himself. Despite the unfamiliarity of language and culture, it is a book that demands attention. No writings have more profoundly influenced the lives of the men and women who have shaped our civilization down the centuries. To read it, especially right through, and perhaps for the first time, is to engage with a piece of living history and to open oneself to a mind-expanding experience.

The contemplative praying of scripture

Brother Ramon

Prayer is simple. It is as natural as breathing and as beautiful as loving. These words *ought* to be true for us all—and they were for me when I was a child and a boy. But what of those of us who have forgotten how to breathe naturally, who are afflicted with respiratory problems, or who have messed up our lives of relating and loving. The analogies no longer hold, though it is not prayer that is complicated—we have become so.

This article is not concerned with corporate and liturgical prayer as in church or group worship, nor with the good but dutiful praying of petition, intercession and thanksgiving. All these are important and part of the growth of the Christian in grace and discipline. But what I want to do here is to introduce you to a basic method by which you can enter into a meditative feeding upon scripture in such openness and simplicity that the Holy Spirit will illumine your mind and move your heart towards the loving contemplation of the mystery of God. This method takes account of the fact that we are incarnate beings, and involves body, mind and spirit in the experience of communion with God.

There are five steps which are simple to uncomplicated people, but which need both fire and perseverance from those of us who have substituted complexity for our early childlike simplicity. They are:

1. Relaxation
2. Respiration
3. Visualization
4. Participation
5. Adoration

The first step, *Relaxation*, refers to the body and the mind. It means that in stillness of body and mind is the preparation for prayer. The second step, *Respiration*, has to do with the Holy Spirit and the human spirit. The word *spiration* means breath, and the Holy Spirit is the breath of God, so that *inspiration* is the human spirit being breathed into by the Holy Spirit. The third step, *Visualization*, is the consequence of such inspiration—it is the enlightenment of the imagination and the heart as you focus upon the text of scripture so that it can yield up its hidden treasure. *Participation* is the fourth step in which you are taken up and into scripture, actually experiencing the biblical incident, or being carried into the context of the passage. The work of meditation is then well under way, and the fifth step, *Adoration*, indicates the mind and heart set upon God, and this opens up a deeper level of understanding and experience which borders on contemplation.

1. Relaxation. Find a quiet place—a church, a room, a prayer-hut or an open-air space. Avoid tight clothing—a track/leisure suit is best and no footgear. Then relax your body. This means finding the right posture, which may be sitting upright on a chair or stool, using a prayer-stool, sitting cross-legged or lying upon the ground (though this may be too soporific for some!). My chosen posture is the prayer-stool kneeling position. Then practice a simple relaxation technique. Begin with the soles of the feet, progressing slowly up to the crown of the head,

Inspiration is the human spirit being breathed into by the Holy Spirit

stretching and relaxing each part of your body, letting go… letting go. It is worth getting some advice and doing some relaxation exercises with a group. The body should be relaxed but alert.

2. Respiration. This second step is the opening of the human spirit to the Holy Spirit, giving attention to your own breathing and to the breathing of the Spirit of God who dwells within you. Breathe from the diaphragm rather than from the top of the chest—belly breathing not shallow chest breathing. Breathing should be easy—easy come, easy go. Practice this for a minute or two until you find your own gentle rhythm. At this point people who practice the Jesus Prayer [1] begin to say the prayer according to their breathing rhythm or their heartbeat. Inspiration is entering into the reality expressed by the hymn 'Breathe on me, Breath of God…'

3. Visualization. This is where you take up the chosen text of scripture and use your sanctified visionary imagination to carry you into the context and teaching of the text. There is the plain meaning to be understood, a clear teaching to be perceived and a number of levels of application which the Holy Spirit may make clear as you

29

enter prayerfully into the passage. This is not Bible study or sermon construction, nor is it an intellectual learning exercise for you do not pray with your brains! It is the offering up of your intuitive vision to the Lord in the light of scripture.

4. Participation. So we are led into the living experience of the fourth step of actually participating in the situation described in the text. If it is a parable or one of the healing miracles of Jesus, then you move from an objective evaluation of the scene, allowing yourself to be ever more deeply drawn into the activity and movement of the story, parable, miracle or Bible situation. You may identify with Abraham being called out from Ur of the Chaldees, Isaac ascending Mount Moriah with his father, Jacob visited by the angelic ladder-vision at Bethel, the boy Samuel hearing God's voice in the night at Shiloh or Joseph and Jeremiah in the pit of abandonment or the well of desolation. In the New Testament, the Gospels and the Acts of the Apostles are full of situations which may become relevant to your own pilgrimage and vocation. As well as giving clear ethical and doctrinal teaching they are full of situations and principles of action which impinge on our personal and corporate lives. St Paul certainly meant that we should enter into the journey of God's people in the wilderness (1 Corinthians 10:1—13), and the writer to the Hebrews certainly calls us to identify with the heroes of faith by the grace of the Spirit (Hebrews 11:1—12:4). Ultimately it is participation *with* Jesus in the words and works of his ministry on earth, and identification *in* Jesus as he enters into the pain and sorrows of Calvary and rises into glory and newness of life. Such identification is the root and sap of Christian mystical theology, exemplified by St Paul in words which would be amazing if they were not so familiar: 'I have been crucified with Christ; it is no longer I who live, but Christ who lives in me; and the life I now live in the flesh I live by faith in the Son of God, who loved me and gave himself for me' (Galatians 2:20).

5. Adoration. This word includes a wide spectrum of experience, from a simple sense of wonder at the beauty and power of Jesus speaking, healing, dying and rising in the Gospels to the timeless, contemplative adoration of God which is beyond language and understanding to us in this life. It is the endless, adoring wonder of those who are caught up into the

> *Out of the experience of depth in prayer and scripture there is the overflow of a life given to God*

very being of God. This is the eternal, trinitarian life of glory and love—the consummation of all things in which rests the stillness and the dynamic of all creation. But even at the elementary and basic level we shall glimpse something of God's glory in the face of Jesus. We shall be struck down with wonder, melted by his love and transfigured in his glory. Isaiah cried out in mortal and spiritual agony at the vision of God; Ezekiel fell down on his face before God's glory; Daniel felt all his strength drain away in the divine confrontation. At one point Peter looked upon the face of Jesus and said: 'Depart from me, for I am a sinful man, O Lord.' And when the three disciples entered into the cloud of glory on Mount Tabor they became speechless with adoring wonder.

I have consciously followed the way of Jesus since I was twelve years old (and unconsciously since my infancy), and some of the most precious and revelatory moments of my life have been the experience of God within scripture. I understand well why Anthony the hermit was smitten by scripture in the third century, sold all his possessions and followed Christ into the desert; why Augustine hearing the word in the garden in Milan in the fourth century suddenly gave up his immoral and restless life and surrendered to God in conversion; why Francis of Assisi, hearing the word of the Gospel in the thirteenth century embraced poverty, celibacy and obedience to live a simple gospel life with his brothers. It was all the result of a meditative listening to the word of scripture while the inspiring Spirit moved within their hearts.

I have laughed and I have wept; I have danced and I have lain smitten on the ground; I have proclaimed with great assurance and been struck to silence—all because of the power of the Holy Spirit within my heart through the word of scripture. And I can translate that last sentence quite easily into the present tense, for it happens now—it happens today, as I hear and understand, and give my mind and heart to obedience and love.

Adoration is the word which covers the whole spectrum of response, for out of the experience of depth in prayer and scripture there is the overflow of a life given to God in words and works of compassion.

If you will give yourself—body, mind and spirit—to God in the contemplative praying of scripture you will find the whole of your being irradiated with the divine compassion, and you will become an instrument of God's peace in our world.

[1] Simon Barrington-Ward, *The Jesus Prayer*, BRF; Brother Ramon SSF, *The Heart of Prayer*, HarperCollins, chapter 11

Brother Ramon is an Anglican Franciscan monk and a hermit. He has written a number of books on prayer.

Editors' Letter

A happy New Year to *Guidelines* readers throughout the world. The readings in this first issue of 1998 have a common theme—the struggle to be faithful to God and his ways. The book of Exodus touches the heart of Israel's faith. Michael Tunnicliffe's notes take us through the stirring account of how Moses, in God's strength, courageously out-faced the wiles of the Egyptian Pharaoh and ultimately led the enslaved Israelites to freedom. Loveday Alexander's readings in 1 Corinthians lay bare the life of a gifted yet troubled Christian community, struggling with the often competing demands of Christ and Corinthian society. There are important lessons here for the way we live out our faith in the real world of today. The story of Jonah is so familiar that its powerful challenge can easily be lost on us. Grace Emmerson's notes help us to read it slowly and meditatively, so that we can reflect on what happens when belief is not put into practice. Michael Wadsworth concentrates on the first seven chapters of Daniel, which largely consist of stories of the Jewish struggle to be faithful to God in a hostile environment. What we learn here about the cost of commitment provides a helpful way into Lent—and, for that matter, into the second half of Mark's Gospel, where Ian Wallis's notes explore the testing of Jesus' faith in his encounters with the Jewish authorities. The story of Jesus' Passion and resurrection underlines the message of Daniel (including the curious vision in chapter 7 which was so important to Jesus), that God stands by those who are faithful to him and vindicates them. As we draw near to Holy Week and Easter, we might wonder what this might mean for us today, living as we do in very different circumstances from those who first read Daniel and Mark. In the weeks after Easter, we return to the exodus theme in the exalted poetry of Isaiah 40–55, with its promise of a new exodus—even more glorious than that of Moses' day—for a people exiled far from home. John Eaton's notes remind us of God's promise to the despairing that he is both able and willing to save, a message to stir our hearts and strengthen our faith.

As always, it has been good to read your letters over the past year. Keep them coming! Editors, authors and BRF staff alike appreciate the feedback we receive.

With all good wishes for the coming year,

Grace Emmerson and John Parr
Guidelines Editors

Exodus 1–15

'Let my people go!' The radical demand of God rings out from these chapters of the book of Exodus. The story of the journey from slavery to freedom has inspired people of faith down the centuries. For a Jewish audience this was the moment the nation of Israel was brought to birth and remembrance of these events at the Passover festival provided a model for future hope, especially when observed in a foreign land. For the early Christians the opening chapters of Exodus were full of symbolic meaning. Jesus had died at Passover time and so the escape from Egypt pointed forward to the greater liberation that Jesus had made possible. For many modern Christians a 'theology of liberation' in which God addresses the poor and oppressed takes its cue from the Exodus story. In various forms the commanding voice of God is still heard, and still inspires. The theme of 'exodus' remains relevant; it is a powerful symbol of the way God is perceived by people of faith.

So for the next three weeks as we explore these chapters we shall focus especially on the pictures of God presented in them.

Week 1—Chapters 1–5—The God who Declares
Week 2—Chapters 6–10—The God who Destroys
Week 3—Chapters 10–15—The God who Delivers

Of the date and place of composition of these stories we cannot be sure. They may well contain material from various periods in Israel's history. However in their final written form they probably come from the period after the exile in Babylon.

The Bible text is quoted from the New Revised Standard Version (NRSV).

5–11 JANUARY   EXODUS 1–5

---

1   In Egypt's land   *Read Exodus 1:1–22*

A new book of the Bible begins, a new chapter unfolds. Yet the story of Exodus is part of the larger story and the opening seven verses remind readers of 'the story so far'. They link this account with the story of Jacob and his household of seventy people (Genesis 46:27) who came down into Egypt. In the intervening years the children of Israel have obeyed the command 'be fruitful and multiply'. Thus in the space between Genesis and Exodus the first part of the promise to Abraham, Isaac and Jacob is fulfilled—numerous descendants, like the stars of heaven. However, the other half of the promise is not yet fulfilled—possession of their own land in Canaan. They are still in a foreign land and are soon to be enslaved there. Will God be faithful to all of his promises?

Pharaoh is not named in the book of Exodus and attempts to identify him have not succeeded. The most common dating places the story at the time of the great nineteenth dynasty in Egypt with Seti I as the Pharaoh of the oppression and his successor Rameses as the Pharaoh of the exodus. This would date the events in the period 1300–1250BC. Other scholars prefer a date 200 years earlier which would be closer to the comment in 1 Kings 6:1 that the period from the exodus to the building of Solomon's temple (around 960BC) was 480 years. In truth the Bible is not primarily interested in exact historical or biographical details. Pharaoh is portrayed in a few words as cunning, devious and cruel, an enemy of God and of God's people. It is ironic that in the book of Genesis Joseph the Hebrew saved Egypt by his policy of storing grain, whereas now his descendants are enslaved building store cities for the Pharaoh who 'knew not Joseph'.

Are the midwives Hebrew or Egyptian? The phrase 'midwives of the Hebrews' could be taken either way. They seem to have good Hebrew names and yet the drama and irony of the story would be enhanced if they were Egyptian. They spin a tale to Pharaoh which is very implausible, but the gullible king believes it. He seems not to be as shrewd as he thinks he is. Surely a really clever king who wanted to keep the birth rate down and yet maintain a building programme would order the destruction of female children, not male! For now the midwives have played their part. For the first time in these opening chapters courageous women play a decisive part in the unfolding story. Other heroines will emerge during the readings this week.

2 Mother, sister, daughter, wife *Read Exodus 2:1–25*

In this chapter the story moves on from the plight of the people as a whole to focus on the way the tragedy affects one particular family. The names of Moses' father, mother and sister are not yet given. This is typical of the style of a folk tale. Similar stories in which a hero is saved in infancy from certain death are found in other neighbouring civilizations.

There is a profound irony in the telling of the tale. The mother does indeed follow the command of the Pharaoh—she casts her child into the Nile. The life-giving river of Egypt has become a river of death for the Israelites. Now it will preserve life once more. The mother makes a papyrus basket for the child. The literal translation is 'an ark of bulrushes' (AV), the same word that is used of Noah's ark. This ark too will be a vessel of salvation. It is ironic too that the saviour of the child should be Pharaoh's own daughter, and that the baby's quick-witted sister should engineer that his own mother should act as wet-nurse, and even be paid for it! Once more the women of Exodus have outsmarted the Pharaoh.

The name Moses (v. 10) is a good Egyptian name meaning 'son' as can be seen in the names of Pharaohs like Thutmose or Rameses. The author of Exodus links it to a Hebrew word that sounds similar, in this case the verb 'to draw out'. Such plays on sounds are common in the Bible.

In verses 11–22 two episodes revolve around the identity of Moses. The adopted Egyptian assumes the role of champion of the Israelites and slays an Egyptian oppressor. Yet he gets no thanks for it and his attempt to identify himself with his own people is met with rejection by the two quarrelling Hebrews. When he goes to the land of Midian he is taken to be an Egyptian. This time though his help is accepted and he finds there a home, a wife and a family. Yet the name of his son Gershom ('stranger there' in Hebrew) testifies to his sense of estrangement.

Finally in verses 23–25 a summary is given of the continuing plight of the Israelites. Despite a new king on the throne there is no relief from oppression. The human Moses has achieved nothing in his clumsy attempt to play the liberator. A new character must enter the drama: a God who hears, remembers, sees and now proposes to act.

3   What's in a name?   Read Exodus 3:1–22

Names and their significance feature largely in today's passage. In 2:18 the priest of Midian who became Moses' father-in-law was called Reuel. In chapter 3 and elsewhere in Exodus he is called Jethro. Likewise the mountain of God is called Horeb here, but in other places the more familiar Sinai is used. These differences may reflect different oral traditions and some scholars believe they indicate different written sources that have been combined in the present Pentateuch. The exact location of Horeb/Sinai is not known—the description in 3:1 is very vague. Once they had left the mountain the children of Israel did not return to it, except for the prophet Elijah in 1 Kings 19. What was important was not the place itself but the revelation that was given there. Since early Christian times the traditional location has been identified as Jebel Musa in the southern Sinai peninsula. Today the ancient monastery of St Catherine's stands at the foot of the impressive mountain.

This chapter recounts one of the supreme moments of revelation in the Bible. To Moses is revealed something of who God is and what God will do. The God who speaks to Moses through the agency of burning bush and angel is the God of past, present and future. Of the past, since he is the God of Moses' own father and of the patriarchs of long ago (v. 6). Of the present because he is the God who now hears and knows what the people are suffering (v. 7). Of the future because he purposes to deliver them from Egypt to a land of their own (v. 8).

What is the name of this God? The name in Hebrew consists of four consonantal letters, YHWH. With vowels added the name was probably pronounced Yahweh. It is explained in this story as being linked to the verb 'to be'. In Hebrew 'he is' or 'he will be' is pronounced 'yihyeh'. So God, the God of the fathers, is now revealed as 'The One who Is' or 'The One who Will Be', or in short as 'I AM'. It is an elusive name, hard to pin down. Some people even think God is telling Moses to mind his own business. The God who encounters Moses is certainly not, however, some static Being, utterly unknowable. He is known by his acts and he will act as deliverer.

'The One Who Is' will bring into being a radically new series of events—but first must overcome the reluctance of Moses himself to play his part.

4 Send somebody else!   *Read Exodus 4:1–17*

Though the God of the Bible calls and commissions, it does not automatically follow that his lieutenants are eager to take up their commission. Among the initially reluctant messengers of God are the pious Isaiah—'I am a man of unclean lips', the timid Jeremiah—'I am only a youth', and the theologically sceptical Jonah. Moses too exhibits a marked reluctance to accept his calling. In chapter 3 he raised two objections: first, 'Who am I that I should go to Pharaoh?' (v. 11), and secondly, 'Who are you?' With the revelation of the divine Name the latter issue is settled, but the former still remains.

Once before Moses attempted to strike a blow for freedom for the Israelites, and it failed miserably. He does not want to be rejected again by his own people. The signs of the staff turned snake, the hand turned leprous, and the Nile turned to blood are given to confirm the authority of Moses. The first and third of these signs are also performed before the Egyptians. The river turned to blood will be the first of the 'smitings' or 'plagues' in Egypt. The fear of leprosy in the ancient world was very great. It is difficult for modern readers, in an age when leprosy can be cured through multi-drug therapy, to realize the shock that lies behind this text.

Though he now has the signs he needs from God Moses still persists in his rejection of the task before him. He is 'heavy tongued' and not even the solemn assurance of the one who made the tongue will convince him. So we are introduced to the eloquent elder brother Aaron who becomes the spokesman for Moses. God's purposes will not be thwarted so easily. Moses was meant to be the mouth of God, now Aaron will be the mouth of Moses. It is Moses however who will instruct Aaron what he is to say—in that sense Moses will be 'as God' to Aaron.

Aaron is designated as the Levite (v. 14) and this reminds us that his role of mediator here points also to the later role of Aaron's descendants as the Levitical priests of ancient Israel. This passage highlights therefore the positive qualities of Aaron as founder of the line of priests who will act as mediators and interpreters of the 'Law of Moses' in later Israelite history.

5   A strange encounter   *Read Exodus 4:18–31*

In a series of swift, if rather disjointed, paragraphs the action moves back from Midian to Egypt. Moses takes with him Zipporah and their sons; however the family are never mentioned in Egypt and in Exodus 18:2 we are told they were sent back at some point to the safety of Jethro in Midian. The motif of the 'firstborn son' (v. 23) is introduced here, which prepares for and explains the severity of the final plague. Finally Moses and his mouthpiece Aaron convey to the Israelites the words of God, and now the people believe and worship God.

On the way between Midian and Egypt comes the strange and terrifying story of the 'bridegroom of blood'. It is very short and leaves many unanswered questions. Why did the Lord attack Moses? Does the term 'feet' here have its normal meaning or, as in some places in Hebrew, is it a reference instead to the genitals? Whose 'feet' are touched, Moses' or his son's? The figure of the Lord seems more like a demon than a god, and some writers see here a very early story from

Israelite or Midianite traditions. As such we can dismiss it as a 'primitive' story, preserved like an ancient fossil in the text. Others try to explain the 'attack' by God as a way of speaking of Moses becoming ill and almost dying. Most commentators agree that it is Moses' failure to circumcise his son, his firstborn perhaps, that leads to the provocation of God. Zipporah's swift action puts things right and confirms the importance of circumcision (v. 26). Note how once more Moses' life is saved by a courageous woman.

As modern readers, do we then dismiss this strange text as a primitive fragment not worth bothering with? Do we pretend such texts don't exist, or wish they would go away? It presents a mysterious, frightening encounter with the divine, similar in certain ways to the better-known story of Jacob wrestling with a man/God at Peniel (Genesis 32:22–32). Perhaps we should take seriously the fact that not all encounters with the divine are either pleasant or easy. Life and circumstances may conspire to assail and attack for no apparent reason. Sometimes the saving grace is in the presence of others whose love rescues us from the nightmare. This text is deep and difficult, but I would not wish to lose it—we need to wrestle with it like Jacob and take risks like Zipporah.

6   Bricks without straw   *Read Exodus 5:1–23*

At the end of chapter 4 it seemed as if Moses' and Aaron's mission would succeed effortlessly as the Hebrews accept these ambassadors of the Lord and believe his word. Such easy optimism receives a severe jolt in this chapter when they encounter the obstinacy of Pharaoh.

Moses and Aaron begin boldly in verse 1, speaking in the name of YHWH God of Israel and demanding a respite for the Hebrews to celebrate a festival in the wilderness. Pharaoh's curt response takes the wind out of their sails! He does not know the name YHWH and has no intention of complying with this strange god's wishes. In verse 3 Moses and Aaron try again, rather more politely this time, requesting a limited three-day journey. Once again they are rebuffed and Pharaoh's response is to make the workload harder. 'Bricks without straw' has become a proverbial phrase. It is the typical response of a totalitarian régime to a defenceless and subject people. The tyrant's brutal dismissal of the pleas for compassion are summed up in the heartless taunt, 'You are lazy, lazy.'

In ancient Egyptian religion the Pharaoh was regarded as the embodiment of the god Re. Therefore this chapter raises pointedly the question: which god will the Hebrews serve—Pharaoh or YHWH? The stage is set for a dramatic struggle. The tension in the story is building towards its climax, and all sense of easy optimism is dashed. Things have only got worse instead of better. The overseers complain to Moses and Aaron (v. 21) and Moses passes on the complaint to God (vv. 22–23), 'You have done nothing at all to deliver your people.' It is time for the deliverer God to produce more than mere words. In modern parlance, let him either 'put up or shut up'!

GUIDELINES

- *Reflect on the role that the women have played in the story so far.*

- *Meditate on God as 'I AM' and recall the 'I am...' sayings of Jesus.*

- *Consider which names or titles of God mean most to you and why.*

- *Try to remember if there have been times when you experienced God as strange or threatening. How did you cope? Who helped you through?*

- *What examples of slavery still exist today? Pray for those who are still enslaved and those who enslave them.*

12–18 JANUARY   **EXODUS 6–10**

1   A second commissioning   *Read Exodus 6:2–30*

By the end of chapter 5 we, the readers, are ready for action. Yet surprisingly the action is delayed and chapter 6 seems to repeat the material covered in chapters 3–5 on the call and commission of Moses. There is a further revelation of the divine name YHWH (vv. 2–9), a repetition of Moses' excuse (vv. 10–13), a reiteration of the command to go to Pharaoh (vv. 26–27), and the reaffirmation of Aaron as the spokesman (7:1–7).

Since the middle of the last century such repetitions have been explained as the result of the final editors of the Pentateuch bringing together various written sources or oral traditions. It has been thought possible to identify these sources not only because of the repetition but also because of distinctive ideas, vocabulary and theology. The use of the different names or titles for God has also been seen as significant. This chapter has been crucial in support of this source theory since in 6:3 it is said explicitly that the patriarchs did not know the special name YHWH. They knew God rather by the name El Shaddai (God Almighty). Yet elsewhere the name YHWH is used regularly in Genesis when God speaks to Abraham, Isaac and Jacob. This theory of sources has not been accepted by everyone; some traditional Jewish and Christian writers argue instead that the different names for God reflect different aspects of God's nature.

For those who accept the idea of different sources, 6:2—7:7 is identified as coming from a late, Priestly source, one that does not use the name YHWH until this point in the Pentateuch. The revelation in verses 2–9 stresses the notion of covenant between God and his people much more explicitly than in chapter 3. The family history in verses 14–25 may indicate specific Priestly interests. After briefly mentioning the lines of the eldest two tribes, Reuben and Simeon, it concentrates on the tribe of Levi, the third-born son of Israel. It highlights the line of Moses and Aaron (v. 20) and includes details of Aaron's descendants (v. 23). So Aaron is more prominent in this genealogy than Moses, and in verse 26 it is Aaron's name which appears first. All this is evidence, it is argued, for the hand of Priestly writers or editors in this section.

2 Signs and wonders   *Read Exodus 7:1–25*

Verses 1–7 involve the commissioning of Moses and Aaron along with mention of the hardening of Pharaoh's heart. Much has been written about this concept and its relation to human free will. If God had hardened Pharaoh's heart then Pharaoh cannot be blamed, and it is cruel to punish him. Such ideas about 'free will' and 'predestination' are not at the forefront of the concerns of the writer of Exodus. The hardening of the heart of Pharaoh indicates that God is in control, he is not taken by surprise when Pharaoh fails to respond. We are in for a titanic struggle, a trial of strength over these next few chapters.

Verses 8–13: At the burning bush Moses' staff turned into a snake (4:3); now we hear that Aaron has such a wonder-working staff too. The term used for snake is different however from that in chapter 4. It is a word that elsewhere can mean 'sea monster' or 'crocodile'. Impressive though this wonder may be, the Egyptian magicians are equal to it. Unfortunately their staffs are no match for Aaron's devouring monster, as the author of Exodus delights in telling us.

Verses 14–25: Since Pharaoh has refused to believe this wonder, his land must suffer the 'smitings' or plagues. The first of these is the Nile turned to blood. Various attempts have been made to explain how, by natural phenomena, the river water can become discoloured and produce the effect of the 'blood Nile'. The other plagues could then follow in natural sequence from the pollution of the water. The book of Exodus is not concerned with such natural explanations. It is a theological work and a theological point is made in striking the Nile. For the river was regarded as a god, a life-giving god. The Lord acts first through Moses' staff and then through Aaron's to make the water unfit to drink. The first plague lasts for seven days and is undoubtedly unpleasant and inconvenient for the Egyptians. Yet the magicians can still reproduce the effect, and Pharaoh himself is untroubled in his palace. There is a Jewish tale that recounts Pharaoh's reply: 'You don't trouble me, for if I can't have water, I'll have wine.' As yet Pharaoh himself remains untouched—but then this is only plague number one.

3 Of frogs and gnats *Read Exodus 8:1–19*

The second and third plagues, of frogs and of insects, can be fitted into a natural sequence. Following pollution of the Nile the frogs leave the waters, and following the death of the frogs the insects begin to breed among their stinking corpses. The description of ten plagues one after the other could become monotonously repetitive. However the author avoids this by describing some plagues at length and others only briefly, and by including particular comments in each of the accounts.

Frogs (8:1–15) It may be significant that among the deities of Egypt there was a frog-headed goddess, Heket. In the first plague Pharaoh remained untouched, but not in this one. The frogs invade even the king's own bedchamber (v. 3 and Psalm 105:30). There is almost a comic element in this description of the ever-intruding frogs. I have a children's story book with a picture of the invasion of frogs which always makes me laugh! The frogs, lovers of wet places, are even found in the dry ovens. Still the magicians of Egypt are able to match this sign, though one wonders whether Pharaoh was pleased to have even more frogs in his land. They are not, however, able to remove the frogs; only the Lord can do that. Pharaoh for the first time appears to waver in his determination, but it is only a bargaining ploy and he immediately goes back on his word.

Insects (8:16–19) In plagues one and two Moses and Aaron struck the waters, now they turn their attention to the dry land. The exact nature of the vermin that plague the Egyptians is not clear, as the differences in the English translations indicate: gnats (NRSV, NIV, GNB), lice (Living Bible), mosquitoes (JB), and maggots (NEB) are all possibilities. While the frogs get everywhere, these insects attack humans and animals particularly. This third plague is unannounced; Pharaoh receives no warning. The same is true of the sixth and ninth plagues and it may be that we should read plagues one to nine as a series of three lots of three.

4 From bad to worse   *Read Exodus 8:20—9:12*

Flies (8:20–32) As in the first plague Moses meets the Pharaoh early in the morning by the river bank. The novel feature introduced in this fourth plague is the distinction between Goshen, where the Israelites have been concentrated since the time of Joseph (Genesis 47:1–6), and the rest of Egypt. The Israelites do not suffer the torment of the flies, or of the later plagues which will culminate in the discriminating work of the angel of death in the climax to the plague tradition. The wily Pharaoh knows he can no longer rely on his magicians so he seeks to bargain. The Israelites can offer sacrifice to the Lord, but only in the land of Egypt, not in the wilderness. The Pharaoh who had begun by saying he did not even recognize the name of the God YHWH now has to acknowledge the power of this deity and asks Moses to pray for him to the Lord (v. 28).

Cattle disease (9:1–7) There is a certain logical progression in this second series of three plagues. After the swarm of flies which spread disease, first the cattle and then humans succumb to infection. Once again the Israelites are distinguished from the Egyptians and their cattle are spared.

Boils (9:8–12) No warning is given for this plague, Moses simply performs the symbolic action with the soot. Now not only the water and the land, but the very air itself is affected. Disease has moved from the realm of cattle to that of humans. The magicians in particular fall prey to the disease. Progressively they have been losing the battle. They held their own for the first two plagues but could not reproduce the third. They were silent for plagues four and five. Now in plague six they themselves are grievously afflicted. This is the last time in the plague cycle of stories that we shall hear of them.

So the second triplet of plagues comes to an end, but the power of one arrogant man still holds out against all reason. The heart of Pharaoh is still as hard as ever.

5 The first casualties   Read Exodus 9:13–35

The third and final series of three plagues, the severest so far, begins at this point. The first series (numbers one to three) caused inconvenience to the land of Egypt and there was even an element of the comically absurd with the frogs. In the second (numbers four to six) first cattle and then humans were afflicted by disease. They became sick, but as yet no one had died. With the third series of plagues (numbers seven to nine) the mood becomes ever more sombre.

Hail (9:13–35) After a number of quite short descriptions of the plagues, the seventh plague of hail is portrayed in much more graphic detail. Moses' early morning address to Pharaoh (as in numbers one and four) is much more extensive and his words bring out the theological significance of the plagues. In addition we are introduced to a further division, not simply between Israelites and Egyptians; now a distinction is made between God-fearing Egyptians and those who took no heed of the warning.

Like the previous plague this one too falls from the sky. Thunder, lightning, hail and rain produce a terrifying spectacle of the awesome power of God. The reason for the specific warning to Pharaoh and his officials is now clear. Man and beast are struck down in the open country (v. 25). For the first time there is loss of life. For the first time too Pharaoh is so badly shaken that he openly admits that he is in the wrong: 'This time I have sinned' (v. 27). So there is some movement in Pharaoh's heart; but Moses has had enough experience of this king by now to doubt the genuineness of his repentance (v. 30).

The brief aside in verses 31–32 explains the different growing seasons for flax and barley, which are harvested first, and for wheat and spelt which come later. The preservation of the latter crops explains how, in the midst of such devastation, there was anything left for the locusts to eat in the next plague.

6 The locust swarm   Read Exodus 10:1–20

Locusts (10:1–20) An important new dimension is introduced in verse 2. The signs that are being performed are not simply for the

43

benefit of Pharaoh and the Egyptians, nor are they even for the benefit of the Israelites in Egypt. Rather they are for the benefit of the future generations. The story must be told to generations yet unborn. The recitation in full of the story of the plagues is still an integral part of the Passover meal or Seder, observed in Jewish homes to this day. There is even a tradition that ten drops of wine are removed from the Passover cup to remind the Jewish people that their joy was achieved only at the cost of the tears of the Egyptians.

Pharaoh's officials now plead with him, in as diplomatic a way as possible, to see sense and let the Israelites go. Moses and Aaron are recalled and diplomatic bargaining begins. Who is to be allowed to go? If Moses takes everyone then it is clear he has in mind a full and final 'exodus', not just a three-day pilgrimage. Pharaoh seeks to limit the numbers to men only, to ensure that the workforce will return. Two wily negotiators face each other but do not spell out their meanings. Pharaoh knows what Moses' words imply, and Moses knows that he knows!

Pharaoh's concession is not enough and the locust swarm descends on the land. The locusts complete the work of the destruction of crops begun by the hail. Now nothing is left and Egypt faces ruin, starvation and destitution. For the second time Pharaoh confesses his guilt, but now, in more anguished terms than before, he pleads for the locust plague to be removed 'just this once' (v. 17).

Things are going from bad to worse in Egypt and the locust plague is an ominous foreshadowing of things to come. The sky and the land turn black with locusts. Yet a still more terrible darkness awaits in the ninth plague. Furthermore, the locust horde meets its end in the waters of the Red Sea or Sea of Reeds. Soon too Pharaoh's host will be no more in those same waters.

GUIDELINES

A number of important questions arise out of the plague story.

- *How far does it help to interpret the plagues as a series of natural disasters that follow a logical sequence? Does this help to explain the story for you or does it seem to explain it away?*

- *Natural disasters are sometimes referred to as 'acts of God'. Is this appropriate or not?*

- *What does the phrase 'God hardened Pharaoh's heart' mean to you as you read the story?*

- *What picture of the God YHWH emerges from these stories? Does the cumulative series of ten plagues denote a vindictive, cruel God who sends one thing after another? Or does it indicate rather a God patient and long-suffering in the face of human obstinacy?*

- *The God of the whole Bible, both Old and New Testaments, is portrayed as taking sides with the poor, oppressed and marginalized. Does this mean that the God who delivers is at one and the same time the God who destroys? That the God who saves is also the God who smites? What might this mean?*

God of the mysterious Name,
you challenge and confront us when we are complacent and
    self-satisfied,
you call and comfort us when we are dismayed and self-doubting.
Grant us grace to hear your voice
and to heed your words of rebuke and of promise. Amen.

19–25 JANUARY   **EXODUS 10–15**

1   Gathering gloom and final warning   *Read Exodus 10:21—11:10*

Darkness (10:21–29) The plague cycle had begun with a sign against the Nile which was regarded as a god. The most powerful deity of all, however, was the sun god Re. So this ninth sign which blots out the rays of the sun strikes at the very heart of Egyptian belief. The unconquered sun has now been vanquished and the consequences are terrifying. All normal life in Egypt is paralysed. Those seeking a natural explanation for the darkness make much of the unusual expression in v. 21, 'a darkness that can be felt'. It has been suggested that this was a particularly severe sandstorm blocking out the sun. Other commentators have interpreted the darkness psychologically—the Egyptians perceived a darkness which was of their own imagining, of their own fears, while the Israelites continued to experience light.

Pharaoh has to make further concessions. Now all people, including women and children, may leave, but not the animals which were a source of wealth. Moses knows that he now has the upper hand and refuses point blank to accept this compromise. Negotiations therefore break down completely. There remains only the final and most terrifying of the plagues.

Firstborn (11:1–10) Before finally leaving the presence of Pharaoh, Moses warns of the disaster about to fall on Egypt. Right at the beginning of Moses' commission the themes of the 'spoiling' of the Egyptians (3:21–22) and of the death of the firstborn (4:22–23) had been envisaged. Israel as a nation would not depart empty-handed from Egypt. Likewise the Law of Moses would insist that when individual slaves were set free they should be recompensed and not simply sent away empty-handed (Deuteronomy 15:13–16).

Chapter 11 acts as something of a bridge. It looks back over the series of plagues in chapters 7–10, and looks forward to the coming deliverance at Passover to be portrayed in chapters 12–15.

2   Do this in remembrance   *Read Exodus 12:1–28*

With this chapter there is a marked change of style from what has gone before. In place of the narrative style of the plague traditions there are instead instructions, precisely and carefully given. The words of Moses and Aaron are addressed to Israel, and clearly not just to the Israelites who are in Egypt but to all future generations too. These are regulations for ritual observance in the future, not simply a record of a one-off event in the past.

Instructions are given concerning two festivals: Passover on the 14th of the month Nisan, and Unleavened Bread on the 15th–21st. Scholars have detected two different points of origin in ancient cultures for these two ceremonies. Passover with its sacrifice of a lamb or goat has been linked to nomadic customs. In the spring nomads would leave one area of pasture for another, a practice called transhumance. Sacrifices would be offered at this time of danger and uncertainty. For the farmer, however, springtime was the time to harvest the first crop of barley. From these two traditions of the herder and farmer may come some of the ceremonies of Passover and Unleavened Bread. In the Bible however these festivals are linked with the historical memory of the coming out from Egypt. This story must never be forgotten (v. 14).

Remembrance and participation are at the heart of the celebration of Passover to this day. It is not surprising that Christians have, from the beginning, interpreted the death of Jesus using the terminology of Passover. This is not simply because Jesus' death occurred at Passover time, but because the Church perceived a deep theological significance in the connections between Passover and Easter. Thus Jesus is portrayed as the spotless lamb, whose bones are not broken, whose shed blood becomes effective for all humankind. Even the bunch of hyssop in verse 22 finds its way into John's account of the crucifixion (John 19:29). 'Christ our Passover has been sacrificed for us,' declares St Paul (1 Corinthians 5:7). Thus the chapter continues to stir deep memories for both Jews and Christians.

3   A night of watching   *Read Exodus 12:29–51*

The tenth plague and the subsequent exodus are described sparingly. The writer does not dwell on the lurid details—that is not the biblical authors' way. The full horror of the scene is caught rather by the 'loud cry' of verse 30 that echoes all through the land of Egypt. Pharaoh's hard heart is finally broken. All the demands of Moses are met, and as a sign of the complete capitulation Pharaoh even requests a blessing from the servant of God (v. 32).

The Israelites depart in haste—though not without their share of spoil. The story of the dough that did not rise provides an explanation of the rule to exclude all yeast from the house during the feast of Unleavened Bread.

The number who left Egypt seems excessively large—600,000 men, plus women, children and hangers-on (vv. 37–38). No entirely satisfactory explanation has been given for this number. It has been argued that the word 'thousand' refers not to the number 1,000, but to a family or tribal unit. This would give a much small number in total. For the biblical text however the emphasis is on the miraculous delivery, and the huge numbers enhance the sense of the miraculous. Alongside the Israelites there are a motley crew or 'mixed multitude' who take the opportunity to leave Egypt as well. Perhaps the presence of these non-Israelites led to the inclusion of the instructions in verses 43–49 about who was eligible to eat the Passover. Only those who are circumcised and their families may eat of it.

The geographical names in verse 37 and historical note in verse 40 ought to help us to locate the route and the date of the exodus. Unfortunately many of the names given for the route of the exodus cannot be identified exactly. Also, since we do not know the year the Israelites either arrived in Egypt or departed from it, the figure of 430 does not help much. Verse 42 contains a nice play on words. On the first Passover night the Lord kept watch over Israel, it was his 'night of vigil'. On future Passover nights Israel must keep watch, and observe their 'night of vigil' in honour of the one who watches over them. Remember the Psalmist's words, 'He who keeps Israel will neither slumber nor sleep' (Psalm 121:4).

4 The firstborn son   *Read Exodus 13:1–22*

Verses 3–10 re-emphasize the importance of correct observation of the feast of Unleavened Bread. The name Abib (v. 4) was the ancient Canaanite name for the month, and means 'month of the green ears of barley'. After the exile in Babylon the Jews adopted the Babylonian names for the months, hence the alternative name Nisan which is still in use today. There is a strong didactic element in these verses: children are to be instructed in the meaning of the story from generation to generation. The 'sign on hand and forehead' (v. 9) was interpreted literally in later Judaism. Small boxes with sacred texts inside called phylacteries were worn and are still used in Orthodox Judaism.

Verses 11–16 concentrate on the law of the firstborn. The death of the firstborn of Egypt raises questions about the firstborn of Israel. All life belongs to God and should be offered back to God, especially the life of the firstborn. There is evidence that human sacrifice did exist in the ancient world. The Hebrews however regarded the practice with horror. So these laws provide a method by which human beings can be ransomed by the substitution of another living creature. If this sounds alien and 'primitive' it is worth remembering that much Christian theology has used this idea of 'ransom' and 'substitution' to speak of the meaning of the death of Christ, the Lamb of God. By the death of the firstborn Son of God we have been redeemed. As St Paul comments, 'you were bought with a price' (1 Corinthians 6:20).

Verses 17–22 describe the beginning of the exodus march. To get from Egypt to Canaan the easiest and most direct route is along the coast road up towards Gaza. However this was a military road, well fortified by the Egyptians. So God leads the Israelites by a circuitous route towards the south-east on the way to the Sinai peninsula. For God has declared that before entering the land of promise Israel must first worship at the holy mountain (3:12). The pillars of cloud and fire symbolize the active, guarding presence of the Lord. Despite the hasty departure there is still time to bring the body of Joseph for burial in the land of promise, in accordance with his dying wish (Genesis 50:25).

5 Through the waters *Exodus 14:1–31*

The Hebrew name for the place where God rescued his people is Yam Suph or Sea of Reeds. Since the time of the translation of the Old Testament into Greek in the third century BC this has been interpreted as the Red Sea. Most modern commentators, however, think some other stretch of water is meant. While some have identified the location as the area of Lake Sirbonis on the Mediterranean coast, the vast majority think of the area of marshes around the Bitter Lakes. We must accept however that theology, not geography, is uppermost in the mind of the author of Exodus.

Once again Pharaoh's heart is hardened and he runs true to form. So too do the Israelites, who at the first sign of trouble turn with bitter recriminations on Moses (vv. 10–12). The grumbling of the people against Moses will pursue him for the next forty years in the wilderness. The point to make here, however, is that it is not Israel's courage or fortitude that wins the day. The battle belongs to God alone and to none other: 'The Lord will fight for you, you only have to keep still.'

Attempts to explain the phenomenon of the parting of the waters run the risk of becoming unconvincing rationalizations. The story depicts both natural events (the east wind pushing back the sea) and supernatural ones (walls of water on either side). The important thing is that what happened at the Sea of Reeds became absolutely central to the faith of Israel. This was *the* saving event to which prophets and psalmists would continually return. Here Israel as a nation was born.

Israel passes from slavery to ultimate freedom and all the tyranny that Pharaoh represents is swept away. In the waters of the sea evil is swallowed up and Israel emerges through the parted waters as newly born. These are waters of destruction and waters of new birth. So too Christian interpreters, theologians and songsters have seen the waters of the Red Sea as a foreshadowing of the mighty waters of baptism. Passover and Easter are linked not just by being at the same season of the year; they share basic themes of liberation and renewal.

6 Victory song *Read Exodus 15:1–27*

In verses 1–12 we find the oldest of the songs sung in praise of the Lord's victory at the sea. It may be very old indeed. Comparing it with ancient examples of Canaanite poetry, some scholars date it as early as the twelfth century BC. If this is so then the Song of the Sea may be among the most ancient portions of the Bible.

In the ancient world chaos was often pictured as a watery ocean that had to be stilled by the Creator. In this early poem some of these mythic elements persist. Creation and deliverance merge here. In verse 8 the waters of the subterranean deep once more obey the Lord God as they did at the dawn of creation. The link between exodus and creation is brought out even more starkly in Isaiah 51:9–11 where the name Rahab has a double meaning: it represents the monster of chaos and also stands for Egypt as the enemy of the Lord. Myth and history intertwine.

Verses 22–27 pick up the story of the journeying of the people. At a place appropriately called Marah (bitterness) the water is unfit to drink—just like the water of the Nile in the first plague. Will history repeat itself in a series of plagues? By the agency of Moses the people learn the answer, 'No'. The Lord will not bring that series of Egyptian plagues upon his people (v. 26). Instead they learn yet another new name for this God of surprises. He is the Lord 'your healer'.

So finally we take our leave of the Israelites at the fertile oasis of Elim (v. 27), encamped by the palm trees, but with forty years of wandering ahead of them. The God of Sinai still awaits them on their journey.

GUIDELINES

The Song of the Sea in Exodus 15 was only the first of many freedom songs. Christian hymn writers have used the Passover and Red Sea story to speak of God's liberating act in Jesus. None has done so more fittingly than John of Damascus who died around AD750. Here are two examples from his pen.

Come, ye faithful, raise the strain
Of triumphant gladness;
God has brought his Israel
Into joy from sadness,
Loosed from Pharaoh's bitter yoke
Jacob's sons and daughters
Led them with unmoistened foot
Through the Red Sea waters.

The day of resurrection,
Earth, tell it out abroad!
The passover of gladness,
The passover of God!
From death to life eternal,
From earth unto the sky,
Our Christ has brought us over
With hymns of victory.

Further reading

W. Johnstone, *Exodus*, OT Guides, Sheffield Academic Press, 1990

John I. Durham, *Exodus*, Word Biblical Commentary, Word, 1987

1 Corinthians

Introduction: How to be a church

1 Corinthians contains one of the most famous chapters in the Bible (usually read out of context). It also contains an amazing variety of topics as Paul deals with a whole series of practical queries raised by the Corinthian church: money, social status, sex and marriage, food, the position of women, and the role of charismatic gifts in the life of the church. The letter thus gives us a 'fly-on-the-wall' insight into the process of learning to become a church, at a time when the New Testament did not exist, when there was no church hierarchy, no theological colleges or Christian bookshops. Any questions that arose (and there were plenty) had to be thought through for the first time. So we see Paul setting out with an engaging honesty to work out some answers to the questions raised by the Corinthians (questions to which he does not always have a definitive answer: cf. 7:10, 12). And we see this young church at Corinth, 'warts and all', struggling to formulate questions and deal with day-to-day problems. They were not perfect, as we shall see: in fact this church seems to have caused Paul as much trouble as all his other churches put together. But if they had been, we would not have had the letter—and we might have been able to get away with thinking that it was somehow straightforward and easy to be a Christian 'in those days'.

First-century Corinth was a bustling commercial centre, funnelling trade through from the eastern Mediterranean to the Adriatic and Rome. It had two ports, Cenchreae and Lechaeum, one on each side of the isthmus. It has a reputation as the 'Sin City' of the ancient world which may not be deserved (cf. Murphy-O'Connor)—or at least no more than any other seaport, then and now. Above all, it was a cosmopolitan city with a constantly shifting population of merchants and businesspeople, bringing a regular influx of new ideas and new religions. However Paul is not addressing the city but 'the church of God in Corinth' (1:2), a church which is less than ten years old (see Acts 18 for its foundation story), yet conscious of a new identity as a distinctive group within the city. And the questions they raise are not about how to become a Christian, but about how to go on being a Christian—in other words, the kind of questions that concern us all, about the practicalities of living the Christian life in the real world which we all inhabit.

Of course our world is very different from theirs on the surface, and some of the practical problems they faced have to be translated so that we can appreciate their impact. But overall I believe that today's churches, as we move into the post-Christian society of the twenty-first century, can learn a lot from eavesdropping on the Corinthians' dialogue with Paul. ('Eavesdropping', however, creates its own problems: reading Paul's letters is like listening to one half of a telephone conversation and trying to reconstruct what the other party is saying.)

---

26 JANUARY–1 FEBRUARY 1 CORINTHIANS 1:1—6:20

1 Consider your call   *Read 1 Corinthians 1:1–9; 16:1–24*

Paul is going to have some fairly negative things to say to this church. So it is important at the outset to get straight all the positive things which are also true about them, and which remain true despite their problems—the things which make this group of people a church, in fact the things which make any group of people a church. This opening section reminds the Christians at Corinth of five key **foundation stones** of their faith, and each one establishes a point which is going to be crucial in the argument to come.

- *They are a group of people **called by God**. Calling is about naming—picking out the individual in the crowd. The Christian life begins with an encounter at the deepest level of identity (cf. Isaiah 43:1–7). But the initiative is God's: it is God's sovereign choice which takes a persecutor and turns him into an apostle (v. 1), or takes a motley collection of individuals and turns them into 'the church of God in Corinth' (v. 2).*

- *They are **called in grace** (v. 4). 'Grace' is a favourite word of Paul's: it stresses that God's call is a gift (the words are linked in Greek), or rather a shower of gifts, poured out on the undeserving. So Paul can describe this young church, without any irony, as 'enriched in every way' (v. 5) and 'not lacking in any spiritual gift' (v. 7). This is a church humming with activity and bursting with life—though not always in the right direction.*

- *They are **called to be holy** (v. 2). Being 'holy' is part of the process of becoming a church—forging a new, distinctive identity which sets* *this group of people apart from their neighbours, almost as a 'third race' (1:22–24). How this works out in practice is a large part of what the letter is all about—with some surprising answers, as we shall see.*

- *They are **called in hope** (vv. 7–8). Paul's preaching always emphasized the future aspect of Christian belief, and the final section of the letter deals with this in some detail (chapter 15). Christian hope, however, doesn't depend on our own faithfulness but on God's (v. 9): grace is not just there at the beginning of the Christian life, but is a constant source of strength and renewal (v. 8).*

- *And finally: they are **called into fellowship** (v. 9). Being a Christian means being called into a relationship with Christ. But that vertical relationship also involves a horizontal relationship with other Christians: it's not just a private spiritual experience. Being a church means being called to be part of a team—called to a journey, not alone, but in 'the blessed company of all faithful people' (v. 2). The collection for Jerusalem (16:1–4) and the greetings from other churches (16:19–20) reinforce this wider horizon at the end of the letter.*

2 Wisdom human and divine   *Read 1 Corinthians 1:10—2:10a*

The problems in this church are evident right from the beginning (vv. 10–11). Paul's opening salvo is a dramatic appeal for unity, not as some kind of theoretical ideal but as a thoroughly practical necessity. This tiny church (Romans 16:23 implies they can still all fit into one house) is less than ten years old, yet it is already splitting into factions attached to different preachers (1:12). Paul deals with this first problem through chapters 1–4; but he begins with an apparent digression on the task of the preacher.

Chloe's people may have thought they were doing Paul a favour in telling him that there was a 'Paul party' among the factions in Corinth (1:11–12). Building up a loyal following was one of the expected rewards of a successful teacher in the Greco-Roman world; and there were many such teachers, travelling from city to city to display their professional skills in philosophical debate and dazzling oratory. This was 'wisdom', and in Paul's world it meant power and status. This was probably what the Corinthians expected in their preachers, and they may well have found such skills in Apollos (Acts 18:24–28).

For Paul, this attitude (however flattering) shows a fundamental mis-apprehension about what it is that lies at the root of the Christian's faith. Is it **baptism**? Not if that means attaching one's loyalty to the person who performed the ceremony (vv. 13–16). Is it **preaching**? Not if that means being impressed with the professional skills of the speaker. The Church's foundations rest not on the preaching of the cross but on **the cross** itself (v. 17). This is why Paul was careful to avoid any ostentatious display of rhetorical skill in his initial preaching in Corinth (vv. 1–5), and why he so deprecates any attempt to set up a 'Paul party'. The gospel is all about reversal, about the overturning of the world's standards and status symbols (vv. 18–28: cf. 2 Corinthians 5:16). But for this message to have its full effect it must be proclaimed in weakness, in fear and trembling, in naked reliance on the power of God (vv. 3, 5).

Not that 'the word of the cross' is devoid of wisdom: but it is a hidden wisdom, inaccessible to the status-obsessed wielders of earthly power (vv. 6–8). Thomas Merton's autobiography recalls how, as an intellectual young New Yorker, he tried to read the Gospels but was baffled by them because 'they were too simple for me'. Wisdom, truth, unsearchable riches are all there (v. 9): but in order to learn this 'spiritual' language we must first abandon all our pretensions and be prepared to begin again at the bottom.

3   Building the Church   *Read 1 Corinthians 2:10b—3:23*

Up to this point in the letter, Paul's Corinthian hearers may well have been congratulating themselves. True, Paul has reminded them of their own humble and insignificant origins (1:26–27): but how things have changed! This group of 'mere nothings' has been chosen by God 'to overturn the existing order' (1:28, NEB). It has privileged access to the mysteries of the divine wisdom (2:6), with the promise of infinite riches 'revealed to us through the Spirit' (v. 10). This is heady stuff, and the key, surely, is the Spirit (vv. 10–16). That's what makes the difference between 'us' and 'them', between the world outside, baffled by the intricacies of the divine plan, and those inside the Church, who speak 'in words found for us not by our human wisdom but by the Spirit' (v. 13)—and the Spirit is something on which the Corinthian church feels itself an authority (see chapters 12–14).

It comes as a shock, then, when Paul rounds on his hearers at 3:1ff and tells them that, far from being a privileged élite with access to the secrets of divine wisdom, they are on the level of a spiritual kindergarten, still living 'on the purely human level of your lower nature' (3:3, NEB). There is nothing spiritual about the partisanship of the rival supporters of Paul or Apollos (v. 4), in fact it reveals a damaging confusion about the real foundations of the Christian life. There is no way in which Christ can ever be seen as one teacher among many (1:12–13): Paul, Apollos, and the other teachers are simply 'God's agents in bringing you to faith' (v. 5), and must never become a cause for pride in human 'wisdom' (vv. 18–23).

The paired metaphors of the gardener (vv. 6–9) and the architect (vv. 10–17) bring the point vividly to life. Teamwork is essential in both: many different skills go into planting and nurturing a garden, or planning and constructing a major public building, and the project goes all the better when the different kinds of skill can operate together for the good of the whole. But no amount of gardening expertise can make things grow (v. 7), just as no architect or bricklayer can compete in importance with the foundation on which the whole building rests (v. 11). Note how both metaphors reinforce the horizontal dimension of church life which Paul had stressed in 1:9. To be called into the fellowship of Christ is to be called to be part of a larger structure: which is one reason why 'splits' or 'cracks' (*schismata*, 1:10) are too dangerous to be ignored.

4 Leadership and status   *Read 1 Corinthians 4*

Chapter 4 ties together the varied themes of this opening section and provides a bridge to the next.

- *The sombre warnings of 3:12–15 highlight the responsibility borne by those who preach or minister within the Church. No one can tamper with the foundation: but shoddy workmanship will not survive the fire of Judgment Day. Paul is fully aware that his own work as a 'steward of God's secrets' (vv. 1–2) stands subject to that final judgment (v. 5). Paradoxically, however, this does not make him any more willing to be prejudged by his correspondents, or by any other human court (vv. 3–5). The apostle, like the steward, is answerable only to the head of the household: he will not submit his ministry to the partial or premature judgment of those he regards as his spiritual children (vv. 14–15).*

- *But Paul's primary concern here is not to defend his own reputation (though we can detect a real sense of pain behind the carefully chosen words). The case of 'Paul v. Apollos' is simply a worrying example of a deeper problem within the church (v. 6). The Greco-Roman world was obsessed with status: setting up comparisons between one preacher and another simply meant carrying that obsession over into the Christian life. Paul's gospel of reversal had obvious attractions for those who felt themselves to be at the bottom of the pile (1:26–28), but they were missing the point entirely if they felt that their new status in Christ entitled them to lord it over others (vv. 8–13). Paul's catalogue of what it really means to be 'called to be an apostle' introduces a theme to which he returns repeatedly in his second letter to the Corinthians (cf. especially 2 Corinthians 10–13); clearly it was a lesson this church found it hard to take on board. Here, at the beginning of the correspondence, the tone is exasperated, but affectionate: can they really not see the point?*

- *So this first section develops two of the foundational themes evoked in the letter's opening paragraph: being a church rests on **God's call** and **God's grace**. The gifts which God showers on the Church, and which have made such a difference in the lives of the Christians in Corinth, are just that: gifts, tokens of divine grace, not status symbols to be boasted of (vv. 7–8, cf. 1:29–31). Being 'puffed up' with an over-inflated idea of one's own importance is something this church seems prone to (vv. 6, 18, 19; 5:2). Paul's claim that everything is now different 'in Christ', if it is to be taken seriously, must do more than just change the names of the people at the top.*

5 Called into holiness   *Read 1 Corinthians 5*

'Consider your call,' Paul says to the Corinthians—and one vital aspect of this is the **call to holiness** (1:2). Chapters 5–7 deal with a series of problems (largely but not exclusively sexual) all linked one way or another with this concept. They illustrate vividly the struggle to work out principles of Christian living on the ground for a community committed to holiness but living and working with colleagues, friends and family who had no such allegiance. They also give us a fascinating insight into Paul 'doing theology on the hoof', in a situation which he himself felt to be strictly temporary (7:29–31).

The essential background to this section is the Old Testament concept of the people of God as a holy community. 'Holiness' in the Old Testament primarily means 'set apart for divine service': **holiness is where God is**. Compare Exodus 19, where the people must be 'consecrated' (i.e. made holy) before they can approach the glory and terror of

Mount Sinai. Leviticus describes a whole system of consecration, in which certain people, places and objects are declared 'holy to the Lord'. This is then extended to the concept of holy behaviour as something which marks out the whole people and sets them apart from the rest of the world (Leviticus 20:22–26). Thus in this chapter, it is not only the specific Old Testament Law which Paul invokes (v. 1; cf. Leviticus 18:8), but his whole manner of dealing with the offence is rooted in the Old Testament understanding of the holy community. 'Delivery to Satan' (v. 5) recalls the penalty of exclusion from the community (Leviticus 18:29) and the scapegoat ritual (Leviticus 16:20–22), while verses 6–8 invoke the Passover ritual, with its powerful symbol of the cleansing out of *chametz* (leaven or yeast: Exodus 12:15–20).

Readers today might be more familiar with the image of bacteria infecting a healthy organism. Paul's overriding concern is for the health of the community: sin is seen as a kind of infection which will, if allowed to, invade and undermine the whole body. Holiness is viewed here in an essentially defensive way: but defence is not simply a matter of drawing lines around the community. This is not a group which has to withdraw into the desert to protect itself. Just as a healthy person can shrug off any amount of infection in the working environment, so the church need not fear everyday contact with pagan society (vv. 9–10). What is dangerous—and Paul's strong words make it clear that he took the issue very seriously—is sin *inside* the community, unacknowledged and undetected (vv. 11–13), which is why the church cannot afford any self-satisfaction with regard to its own moral standards (vv. 2, 6a).

6 Holiness matters *Read 1 Corinthians 6*

Chapter 6 begins with a brief 'sandwich' digression on the question of lawsuits within the community (vv. 1–6). Paul seems to accept without question that the church has both the competence and the responsibility to act as a civil court in cases of dispute between members, just as the Jewish community did (and still does). There is little point in indulging in eschatological* pipe dreams of judging the world if one is not prepared to exercise moral judgment within the more mundane circumstances of everyday life (vv. 2–3). Not that this is the whole story: verses 7–8 give a hint of the gospel teaching on forgiveness which surfaces again in chapter 13.

* from the Greek *eschaton*, 'end'; eschatology refers to beliefs about the end of this world order and the coming of God's new creation.

Paul's immediate concern, however, is to underscore the importance of maintaining the highest ethical standards within the Church: **holiness matters**. Christians who commit fraud or injustice are not only wronging their brothers and sisters but betraying the standards of the holy community into which they have been redeemed (vv. 9–11). These standards are defined in general terms almost wholly reliant on traditional Old Testament morality: Paul's radical attitude towards the law on circumcision does not mean any relaxation of the traditional ethical code in sexual matters. But this may explain some of the Corinthians' confusion: 'Everything is permissible' (v. 12) may be a Corinthian paraphrase of a piece of Pauline radicalism: Christians are not under the Law, so there are no more rules. The effect is to reduce the concept of holiness to a purely 'spiritual' level which has nothing to do with the way Christians actually behave: and this is a road down which Paul refuses to go. His answer is an uncompromising restatement of the highest standards of sexual morality, and shows an equally uncompromising commitment to the importance of the body in Christian ethics. There is no room for double standards here, either for the community (chapter 5) or for the individual. Sexual relations with a prostitute entail exactly the same kind of commitment as the sexual relationship which forms the foundation of marriage (v. 16). The difference is that the one is a dangerous compromise with sin which allows impurity to invade the Christian body, while the other is a fulfilment of divine law which has the opposite effect—as we shall see in chapter 7.

GUIDELINES

- *Whose problem is Paul really talking about in chapters 1–4? Certainly he highlights a long-standing **problem for preachers** in the temptation to court popularity, to rejoice (secretly, of course) when our teaching is preferred to another's, to take an improper pride in seeing 'results'. 'Boasting' is one of the most insidious temptations in the service of God, and it's one that Paul was constantly aware of. How can we learn a proper rejoicing in the exercise of a God-given talent without falling into the trap of forgetting the Giver?*

- *But there is also a **problem for churches**, where there is a constant temptation to become partisans of a particular preacher or cause. It is not difficult to think of parallels in today's Church where the success of a 'star' church leader has turned disastrously into a* personality cult. 'Causes' within the Church can have the same effect, where devotion to a particular political issue, however right and proper in its place, can swallow up a disproportionate amount of spiritual energy. It's worth remembering the background to the 'parties' in Corinth. Paul had real disagreements with Peter over a serious matter of principle, and did not scruple to tell him so (Galatians 2:11–14). But he totally rejects the idea that this would justify the Corinthians in setting them up as rivals: their unity in Christ works at a much more fundamental level. What parallels can you think of for this situation today, and how can we keep the balance between sticking up for our principles and recognizing a deeper unity?

Father, we thank you for your Word. We thank you for the church at Corinth, which had the determination to ask questions—and for the apostle Paul, who had the courage to try to work out answers. Give us both the courage to differ and the grace to recognize our fundamental unity in Christ, who died so that those who were once strangers should be reconciled in a single body to God through the cross.

2–8 FEBRUARY   1 CORINTHIANS 7:1—11:16

1   Holiness on the offensive   *Read 1 Corinthians 7:1–16*

Up to this point, Paul's treatment of sexual matters is probably more or less what most people expect: conservative, uncompromising, negative. It builds up a picture of a church on the defensive, putting up barriers to protect itself from pollution—and particularly, a church on the defensive about sex, as if sex itself is the main problem. And the beginning of chapter 7 appears at first sight to justify this impression (as well as embodying all that most people like least about the apostle Paul). But appearances can be deceptive: this chapter actually contains some of the most positive statements about sexual relationships in the whole of the New Testament, as well as some very positive statements about singleness. Part of the problem is that we don't always know exactly who is saying what. Chapter 7 starts with a reference to a letter written by the Corinthians to Paul, and many scholars believe that the words which follow in verse 1 are actually a quotation from their letter on which Paul is commenting. Certainly it is clear that the whole agenda in this chapter is driven by the Corinthians' concerns.

Paul's negative attitude in chapters 5–6 arose in response to an over-spiritual permissiveness, which failed to take seriously the sins committed in the body. But this defensive attitude to holiness can itself lead to the opposite error, which is what Paul deals with in chapter 7. If the first can be summed up as 'Anything goes', the second can be caricatured as 'No sex please, we're Christians.' This is clearest in the question of mixed marriages (vv. 12–16). If holiness matters (and if it is important, as Paul says, in the body and not just in the soul), how does this affect Christians who are married to unbelieving partners? Don't these unions also create a channel for impurity to enter the body of Christ (cf. 6:15)? Clearly this was a matter of deep concern to many Christians in Corinth. But Paul's extraordinary answer is that within marriage, the sexual relationship actually has the reverse effect: far from threatening the holiness of the community, sex within marriage reverses the purity force field. Holiness is not a weak, defenceless quality which needs to be protected against infection. On the contrary, it's an active, vital force which 'infects' (or perhaps better protects) the unbelieving partner in the marriage, and even the children (v. 14). Quite what this means theologically is perhaps something we could reflect on more than we do. Perhaps C.S. Lewis has something like this in mind when he makes Screwtape complain of a Christian household that 'The whole place reeks of that deadly odour... Even guests, after a week-end visit, carry some of the smell away with them.'

2 Holiness is where you are   *Read 1 Corinthians 7:17–40*

The key passage for understanding this chapter comes in verses 17–24, which enunciate the general principle that we are to follow Christ in the situation in which we are called. The image of the 'call' can of course be misleading, especially if we take the Gospel stories of the call of the disciples (e.g. Mark 1:16–20) as a literal norm. It is clear that many early Christians did take it literally, giving up their jobs (1 Thessalonians 4:11–12), family responsibilities and marriages to follow Christ. But Paul makes it clear that we are not called to abandon our normal everyday activities in order to achieve a holy lifestyle (unless they are inherently sinful)—any more than we are called to withdraw from the world (5:10). We are called to be holy in our everyday situation, whatever that may be. Distinctions of gender, class and race may seem very important: but in the perspective of eternity they pale into insignificance (though there is no reason to refuse the option of changing one's status if the opportunity arises: 7:15; 7:21b, NEB, RSV).

This is why Paul seems to be saying so many contradictory things in this chapter. Is it better to be married or not married? Essentially, it doesn't matter—as long as you do the job properly.

- *7:1–11: is it OK to be single (which is what v. 1b really means)? Paul's answer is clearly 'Yes'—in fact it's the state he is in himself (vv. 6–8). And, incidentally (and much more revolutionary in Paul's day), it's OK for a woman to be single, whether unmarried or widowed (vv. 8, 34, 40): in fact this chapter has been called a charter for the single.*

- *vv. 25–40: should a Christian get married? 'Stay as you are' is all very well, but what if you're engaged? Paul himself clearly thinks it's better not to get entangled with all the responsibilities of marriage (vv. 28–35), especially in view of the present 'necessity' (v. 26, which probably refers to the stresses of living in the end-time). But anyone (man or woman, Paul is careful to specify) who wants to get married should do so: 'it is no sin' (vv. 28, 36–38).*

- *But if you are married, then for heaven's sake do the job properly! The prime concern for the married is pleasing their partner (vv. 32–34: and note that this applies just as much to the man as to the woman). Be realistic, Paul says: this can cause a conflict of interests (he may be thinking particularly of the life of a travelling missionary like himself). But the implication is clear that this mutual attentiveness to the partner's needs is a right and proper part of marriage (or even engagement: v. 36)—and that includes being attentive to the partner's sexual needs (cf. vv. 2–5: note again that this applies equally to both partners). Some Christian couples in Corinth clearly wondered if the need to be holy meant giving up sexual activity even within marriage. Paul's answer is clearly 'No': maybe for a short time (by mutual agreement), but not for long, and certainly not permanently.*

3 Food offered to idols *Read 1 Corinthians 8*

In chapters 8–10 Paul deals with a new topic (almost certainly another question raised by the church), that of 'food offered to idols' (v. 1)—again with a 'sandwich' digression in chapter 9. Once again, the problem concerns the boundaries of the holy community and its relationship with the pagan world in which it lives. The Corinthians knew that becoming a Christian meant turning away from 'dumb idols' to serve the one living and true God (12:2). The principle was clear: but in practice it was not always easy to be sure where 'idolatry' began. Meat bought in the market place (10:25) might have been slaughtered as part of a pagan religious ceremony: should a Christian eat such meat? Dinner parties were often held in temple dining rooms (v. 10): should a Christian accept such invitations? The issue is outside the experience of most Western Christians today (though it is well to remember that it is very much alive in many churches in Africa and south-east Asia): but there are other, equally shadowy issues on which Christians in the West hold different opinions: Hallowe'en provides a good example (or the National Lottery, perhaps?).

The line of Paul's argument is confusing because he seems to be allowing for more than one possible position on the issue: but the underlying thrust is clear enough. On the theoretical side, Paul is quite ready to admit that there may be a range of valid Christian answers. One is the strong-minded, rationalistic position outlined in verses 4–6, which may be summarized as follows:

- *There is only one God.*

- *Therefore 'idols'—i.e. pagan gods—do not exist.*

- *Therefore idols cannot spoil perfectly good food created by God.*

Paul seems implicitly to approve of this approach, and makes it the basis for allowing the eating of market place meat in 10:25. But there is also a 'weaker' position (v. 11) which cannot rid itself of the sense that pagan gods exist, and therefore that the Christian cannot participate even in apparently harmless social activities without compromise (vv. 7–10). To such a person, eating meat which might have come from a pagan sacrifice (or attending a social event in a temple) will always *feel* wrong, whatever rational arguments may say to the contrary: and this can only have the effect of desensitizing the conscience so that it fails to do its job when the really important issues come along.

Paul does not attempt to arbitrate between these two views on purely intellectual grounds: knowing the right answer is not the whole story (v. 2). The real issue, he insists, is not which view is right intellectually but which view takes account of the interests of other members of the community: 'knowledge' which has such a catastrophic effect on the faith of a fellow Christian (vv. 9–13) cannot 'build up' the church. The touchstone for Christian action is not knowledge but love (vv. 1, 3).

At first sight, this chapter seems to be introducing an entirely new topic, and many commentators have seen it as a digression in which Paul turns aside to defend his own apostleship. But in fact (as is now widely recognized), apostleship is simply introduced as an example of the potential conflict between individual rights and responsibility to the community. The idol foods dispute, as Paul sees it, can be expressed as a conflict between the 'knowledge' of the intellectually superior (who may also be the better-off members of the church) and the 'love' which concentrates on building up the church. But it can also be seen in terms of Christian 'liberty' (8:9) or 'rights' (9:4: the Greek word *exousia* underlies both verses)—liberty from outworn rules and superstitions, the right to eat what one likes (8:8). It is an issue dear to Paul's heart: cf. Galatians 5:1. Yet in chapter 9 he uses himself as an example to argue that 'rights' must sometimes be subordinated to responsibilities.

The first part of the chapter (vv. 1–12) advances a series of arguments for the rights of an apostle, and in doing so sheds a fascinating sidelight on the finances of the early church. Apostles (and their wives) have a right to be supported by the churches in their full-time travelling ministry. The case seems unassailable, buttressed by arguments from natural justice (vv. 7, 10), from Old Testament Law (vv. 8–9), from the practice of the temple (v. 13), and from Jesus himself (v. 14—one of the rare occasions when Paul actually quotes a saying of Jesus). Although there was no full-time local ministry in Paul's day, it is clear that there was a developed support network for the travelling apostles, and that Peter and others made good use of it (v. 5). Yet—and this is the point of the digression—Paul chose not to use this right where he felt it might hinder the advance of the gospel (vv. 12, 15–18; cf. Acts 18:1–3). There is no dispute that the right exists: but in this case it is subordinated to the greater good of the gospel (vv. 19–23). Quite *why* Paul refused to accept support from the Corinthian church we shall never know (though it became a cause of friction later: cf. 2 Corinthians 11:7–11). But it is clear that he felt strongly that in this case, accepting financial support would have compromised his primary task of preaching the gospel: possibly the richer members of the church were attempting to use their financial power as a means of patronizing and controlling the apostle. Where he does accept support, he prefers to use the language of 'partnership' (Philippians 1:5; 4:14): though even here it is clear that Paul does not find it easy to be dependent on others' generosity. When it comes to asking for money for other people, however, Paul shows no such qualms. Note, for example, the pragmatic arrangements for the collection for the Jerusalem church (16:1–4), an important project in Paul's later ministry which he uses to strengthen the ties between his own Gentile churches and the parent church in Jerusalem (cf. Romans 15:25–27).

5 The dangers of idolatry *Read 1 Corinthians 9:23—11:1*

Apostolic finance was never the real point at issue here: the key to chapter 9 lies in the last few verses, where Paul uses the metaphor of the athlete to remind his hearers that living the Christian life takes both discipline and endurance (vv. 23–27). The metaphor changes in 10:1–10 to the Old Testament story of the exodus and the wilderness journey. This is the story of the 'holy community' *par excellence*, the people of God saved by divine action at the Red Sea, and summoned at Sinai to live a life of obedience, and Paul uses it as a 'type' (Greek *tupos*, NEB 'symbol') for the holy community in Corinth. Neither baptism nor miraculous feeding (vv. 1–14) make the ransomed community immune to temptation (vv. 6–10): there are very real pitfalls along the way, and watchfulness is a constant requirement (vv. 11–13). The argument recalls the building metaphor of 3:10–12, with its warning that shoddy workmanship will not survive the fire of judgment. But Paul's immediate point is to underscore the fact that falling back into idolatry is a real and ever-present danger for these new Christians, as it was for the ransomed people of Israel: and this is the topic to which he now returns (v. 14).

Membership of the body of Christ is expressed symbolically through the sharing of bread and wine at the eucharist (vv. 16–18). By the same token, participating in a pagan sacrifice means entering into 'fellowship' or 'partnership' (*koinonia*) with pagan deities: and this is completely out of the question for a Christian (vv. 19–22). (Paul here follows one persistent strand of Old Testament thinking that since these pagan deities do not exist, this actually means fellowship with demons: cf. Deuteronomy 32:17.) Moreover—and here Paul finally returns to the point from which he started in chapter 8—being a member of the body also brings the Christian into partnership with others who share in the bread and drink from the same cup (v. 17)—and this entails responsibilities as well as rights (10:23–24). The 'strong' position is perfectly correct in itself: meat from the market can be accepted as a gift from God (10:25–26), and social invitations from unbelievers should not be subjected to unnecessary inquisition (10:27). But if somebody else—the host, or a 'weaker' church member—raises the question of idolatry, the issue should be treated with all the seriousness it deserves. In this case, responsibility to the other's spiritual needs takes precedence over our own spiritual liberty (vv. 28–32).

6 Women in the church *Read 1 Corinthians 11:2–16*

The potential conflict between rights and responsibilities also underlies the discussion of women's headgear in chapter 11. In reading this chapter, we need to bear in mind Paul's own teaching that the new creation in Christ meant the abolition of the most deep-seated race, class and gender divisions in ancient society: 'There is no such thing as Jew and Greek, slave and free, male and female: for you are all one in Christ Jesus' (Galatians 3:28). This foundational statement of what it means to live 'in Christ' may well be one of the oldest baptismal formulae of the early Church. It seems to underlie the long discussion of 1 Corinthians 7, which deals with the same three divisions and which is noticeably (and unusually for its time) even-handed in its treatment of the roles of men and women within marriage. The formula itself is repeated in 1 Corinthians 12:13—but, significantly, 'male and female' is now omitted (cf. also Colossians 3:11); and in chapter 11 (and even more in 14:33–35), Paul seems to be dealing with the women in the Corinthian church on a very unequal basis. What is going on here?

One solution is to argue that this new oneness 'in Christ' has a purely spiritual meaning ('in the sight of God'), so that its effects will only be felt at baptism, or perhaps in heaven. But this would be contrary to one of Paul's deepest and most passionate convictions, that what is true 'in Christ' *must* also begin to be true in the everyday life of the Christian community (Philippians 2:5, NEB). This is the whole point of the argument with Peter described in Galatians 2:11–14, and—as we shall see—it is crucial to the argument of 1 Corinthians 11:17ff. In fact it seems most likely that the Corinthian church had taken Paul up eagerly on this point at least (v. 2), so that women were not only praying and prophesying in the church (v. 5: 'praying' here must mean a public activity), but doing so without the headcoverings traditional in ancient society. Why Paul thought this was wrong we don't know: he has not abandoned his view on the mutual interdependence of male and female in Christ (vv. 11–12), and he nowhere states that the women should give up their public roles in worship. The headcovering was also a way of keeping long hair bound up in public, and both were closely connected with the preservation of a woman's reputation for modesty. The freedom allowed to women in the early Church could (and did) attract hostile attention from outsiders, and perhaps Paul felt instinctively that the church's interests were not best served by the public flouting of traditional dress codes.

GUIDELINES

Part of learning how to be a church is accepting that this means a call to maturity, to be 'grown-up in your thinking' (14:20). This means being open to the possibility of change under the guidance of the Spirit. But it also means that we may not always agree with our fellow Christians about the timing and direction of change: in other words, it means being prepared to live in a fellowship where there will not always be total uniformity of opinion (11:19). It also means being prepared to accept that in this world there won't always be easy answers. Living in faith means just that: living in trust, living with a degree of uncertainty. The Bible does not provide a once-for-all, 'no argument' body of knowledge, a detailed set of moral instructions for every eventuality from the first century to the twenty-first, though it does provide core principles as a basis for working out what's right in our particular situation.

- *How can the principle of 8:3 help us in dealing with some of the fuzzier areas of behaviour on which Christians differ today?*

- *'There is no Jew or Greek, there is no slave or free, there is no male and female: for you are all one in Christ Jesus' (Galatians 3:28). The first of these distinctions was the one whose abolition absorbed most of Paul's attention: hence Romans and Galatians. How long did it take for Christians to work out the full implications of the second and the third?*

- *Because of Paul's conviction that he and his churches were living in the last days (cf. the 'we' in 15:52), it is quite difficult to extract from his letters an explicit theology of work. Can we use chapter 7 to help us to work out a sacramental understanding of ordinary Christian living in the everyday world of work and relationships?*

So shall no part of day or night
From sacredness be free
But my whole life, in every step
Be fellowship with Thee.

H. Bonar

1 Discerning the body   *Read 1 Corinthians 11:17–34*

1 Corinthians was written in the late 50s of the first century, and its descriptions of the Lord's supper are therefore among the earliest we possess. Meeting together regularly to break bread and share the 'cup of blessing' was clearly important for the Corinthian church (10:16–17), and the solemn way in which Paul recalls the traditional origin of the ceremony (vv. 23–26) shows that he too took it very seriously. But, like so much else in this letter, it is only mentioned because there is a problem in the church. The Corinthians are in danger of 'desecrating the body and blood of the Lord' by eating and drinking 'unworthily' (v. 27), and this calls for a careful self-examination before the ceremony (vv. 28–32). This is a solemn warning, which all Christians can well take to heart: but what is the particular danger in the Corinthian situation?

As usual, we have to reconstruct the actual situation in the church from the rather meagre clues in the text. In verses 17–22 we meet again the 'divisions' (*schismata*, v. 18) which engaged Paul's attention in chapters 1–4. This time, however, the lines of division are explicitly connected not with rival preachers but with social status. Far from being a shared 'communion' meal, the Lord's supper (*kuriakon deipnon*, v. 20) has degenerated into a series of private meals (*idion deipnon*, v. 21), in which some have too much while others go short (v. 21), and those who arrive early just go ahead (v. 33). We should remember that the church could only meet in private houses at this date, and was therefore dependent on the hospitality of richer members like Gaius (Romans 16:23) who owned a house big enough to host church meetings. In these circumstances, it might have seemed quite normal, according to Roman social custom, that the host would serve a luxurious meal to his friends and social peers and a much meaner repast to his social inferiors (cf. Theissen, chapter 4).

But, social custom or no, such discriminatory eating patterns are not acceptable in the church: whatever members may do in the privacy of their own homes (and Paul does not attempt to legislate for that, cf. v. 34), the 'Lord's supper' does not deserve the name unless it is a real expression of community (v. 20). It is a powerful reminder that Christian fellowship means entering not only into a vertical relationship with Christ (v. 26), but also into a horizontal relationship with one's fellow believers: sharing the body (10:16) also means becoming a member of the body (v. 29). This partnership does not necessarily imply an instant community of interests or opinions (as we saw in chapters 8–10), but it must transcend the natural boundaries of social class, and it must be demonstrated concretely in the ongoing life of the church. (What would Paul think of the traditional expression 'making my communion'?)

2 Spiritual gifts   *Read 1 Corinthians 12:1–26*

The importance of this horizontal dimension in Christian living has emerged in a number of different contexts throughout the letter. Now Paul draws all these threads together in chapters 12–14, which form the letter's fourth major section dealing with the use and abuse of spiritual gifts within the church. The 'body of Christ', of which all believers become members at baptism (vv. 12–13) becomes the controlling symbol in this passage. Paul develops the familiar philosophical metaphor of the body, with its diverse members and organs, to produce a compelling model of diversity within a single, complex organism.

The immediate question concerns the origin of the many spiritual gifts which are clearly manifest in this church (cf. 1:7). Not all spiritual phenomena are the work of the Holy Spirit, and discernment is required (v. 3). No spirit which refuses to acknowledge the lordship of Christ can come from God. The confession that 'Jesus is Lord' is the only secure foundation for leadership, teaching or charismatic gifts within the Church. But what a rich diversity is built on that foundation! Intellectual discernment, powers of healing, charismatic speech and prophecy—all are gifts showered on the Church by God's abundant grace (vv. 4–11), and all are part of the one complex organism (vv. 12–13). It's easy to look at such a richly endowed church and think it has no problems: but the very abundance and variety of these gifts can create temptations for the unwary.

- *There's the obvious temptation of overvaluing one's own gift and looking down on others (v. 21). The body metaphor makes the error of this view clear: very often, it is the least visible parts of the system that are the most important (vv. 22–24).*

- *Then there's the equal and opposite error of undervaluing one's own gift and its contribution to the whole (vv. 15–17). The body's*

*public 'communicators', especially, tend to hog the limelight: but
that doesn't mean that those with other gifts should write themselves out of the script.*

- *There's the temptation to wish that everyone else was the same as
oneself (vv. 18–20). That might make for a cosy clique, but it would
not provide the diversity necessary for the body to function properly.*

- *There's also the temptation to care only about oneself and what
happens to one's own gift (vv. 24–26). In a complex organism,
specialization of function makes each member interdependent with
the others that go to make up the whole. In a healthy church, each
member will be as concerned to develop and nurture the gifts of
others as their own.*

3 All you need is love   *Read 1 Corinthians 12:27—13:13*

This is probably the most famous chapter in the New Testament, but it
is usually read out of context. In fact this is the last of Paul's 'sandwich'
digressions, tying together chapters 12 and 14 and summing up one of
the letter's fundamental themes. The body metaphor of chapter 12 is a
picture which celebrates both unity and diversity. The variety of gifts is
highlighted in the repeated lists of verses 27–30 (cf. also 12:8–10;
Romans 12:6–8; Ephesians 4:11), which show not a fixed hierarchy of
church offices but 'clusters' of gifts in four areas: teaching, miraculous
healing, administration and tongues. But the unity of the body—that
which makes it an organism and not just a miscellaneous collection of
individual talents—resides in something of a quite different order (v.
31), not one gift among others but the 'Way' *par excellence*. Without it,
tongues are no more than the empty clanging of the bronzes for which
Corinth was famous (v. 1). Teaching gifts and wonder-working faith are
'nothing' without it (v. 2). Even the ultimate self-sacrifice (of property
or of life itself), without love, is an empty gesture (v. 3). This is the
invisible mortar which binds the stones together to make the temple
(3:17), the secret of 'discerning the body' (11:29) which encourages
each member to look to the interests of the other (10:24; 12:25–26).

What is this love and how does it work? It is noticeable that Paul says
nothing here about warm feelings and hugs: the real work of love lies
behind the scenes, in the tough and sinewy exercise of forbearance and
hope (vv. 4–7). Many of these attributes are expressed in a negative form,
as if love is constantly having to hold itself back from the cutting com-

ment, the spark of offence, the vanity which maximizes its own achievements ('puffed up' in verse 4 echoes 4:6, 18–19) but notices only the faults of others (v. 5). It is in these everyday battles with self that the struggle really lies, and often it is in our closest relationships that the friction is most obvious. Paul's 'hymn to love' is easy to read, but each item in the list is worth long and prayerful meditation.

The final section of the chapter (vv. 9–13) underlines love's eternal importance: not only is it more important than all the gifts now (vv. 1–3), but it is the only one which will still be relevant in heaven. (If we want to know which of all our Christian activities will survive the fire of judgment (3:12–13), this is a good place to start.) In the light of heaven, even the highest gifts of knowledge and prophecy are put into perspective: Paul himself is aware that all his wisdom will be swallowed up in the reality of God's presence, like a child's perception of adult life or like the fuzzy reflection of a well-loved face which was all you could get in the bronze mirrors manufactured in Corinth. 'Here our knowledge is mediate, the result of inference and instruction; it is partial and confused; a piecemeal succession of broken lights. There it will be immediate, complete, and clear; a connected and simultaneous illumination' (Robertson and Plummer, *ad loc.*). Living in faith, as we do now (v. 13) means living in trust, living with an element of uncertainty. Mercifully (to borrow an anachronistic image from modern technology), the glass which separates us from heaven is one-way glass: we can't see through it clearly from the outside, but we can be seen (v. 12, cf. 8:3). In the last analysis, what really matters is not what I know of God but what God knows of me (8:3, cf. 1 John 4:10–12).

4 Tongues and prophecy   *Read 1 Corinthians 14*

The perspective of chapters 12–13—love as the unifying principle which enables the body to function as an organism—determines priorities in the use of charismatic gifts (tongues and prophecy) within the church. The debate here is not over whether such things should happen. Clearly they do happen, they bring the individual closer to God (vv. 2, 4, 16, 28), and they are to be sought out keenly (vv. 1, 5). Paul himself is happy to exercise the gift of tongues (v. 18). Nevertheless, Paul argues, its role *in the church* (i.e. in public meetings for worship and teaching) should be subordinated to the gifts which 'build up' the life of the community (14:3–12).

These community-building (or 'edifying') gifts are described under the blanket heading 'prophecy'—which here (as most often in the Bible) means not prediction but divinely inspired speech. This chapter gives us a vivid picture of the worship meetings of the earliest Christians. Members contribute as they feel led by the Spirit, in a variety of speech forms: prayer (vv. 14–15); thanksgiving (vv. 16–17); hymns (literally 'psalm', vv. 26, 15); teaching (vv. 2, 26); knowledge (v. 6); revelation (vv. 26, 30). All these contributions, whoever they come from (there is no suggestion of a formal liturgy or leader) have the 'power to build' (v. 3, NEB); they provide 'strengthening, encouragement, and comfort' (v. 3, NIV). They are given primarily for the benefit of the community (v. 22), but they also have the potential to bring conviction to any outsider who should happen to be at the meeting (vv. 24–25).

There is however some need to control this spiritual fecundity. Even prophets are not intelligible unless they speak one at a time (vv. 30–31) and allow time for reflection (v. 29—good advice for preachers!). Tongue-speakers should be limited in number, and followed by interpretation (vv. 27–28). The whole thing should run 'decently and in order' (vv. 40, 33), and should allow room for the exercise of the mind as well as the spirit (vv. 13–19): these are the marks of a mature faith (v. 20).

The two verses on women (vv. 33b–35) are a puzzle. Paul cannot be forbidding all speech to women, since we already know that women join in the activity of praying and prophesying (11:5), and Paul has not done anything to control this except to insist on the wearing of head-coverings. There is some evidence to suggest that these verses were added at a later date when women's roles in the early Church were becoming more restricted: otherwise, we must assume that 'speak' here means 'chatter' or 'ask questions' (cf. v. 35).

5   Resurrection faith   *Read 1 Corinthians 15:1–34*

Paul devotes the last major section of the letter to an impassioned argument against a scepticism which found it impossible to believe in the resurrection. It is comforting in a way to find that there were sceptics in Corinth just as there are today: and these were not unbelievers (as in Acts 17:32) but members of the church ('some of you' 15:12). It is naïve to think that faith was somehow 'easier' in the ancient world: the supernatural claims of the Christian faith have never been easy to assimilate. For educated Greeks, the idea of the resurrection of the body—as opposed to the immortality of the soul—may have caused particular difficulties.

The summary of the gospel with which Paul begins (vv. 1–11) is a valuable witness to the earliest Christian preaching (at least a decade earlier than our written Gospels), and it is important to note that this is not some Pauline idiosyncrasy but the common tradition passed down and proclaimed by all the apostles (vv. 3, 11). The core of the gospel is story, a series of events that took place at a particular point in time (vv. 3–4). These events in their turn form part of an older story, the age-old history of God's dealings with humanity ('according to the scriptures'). But the key events belong to recent history, so recent that many of the witnesses are still alive (vv. 5–10): the effectiveness of gospel preaching must rest on the testimony of first-hand experience.

None of this, it seems, was contested by the Corinthian sceptics: this preamble is all part of the common core of belief. What is in doubt is the consequences of all this for the future of the believer (vv. 12–19). Paul taught that Jesus' resurrection was only the 'first fruits' (v. 20) of a general resurrection at the end of time, part of the whole eschatological complex of events which included judgment and the final defeat of death (vv. 20–28). Getting this right is not simply a matter of abstract doctrine. 1 Corinthians is a very pragmatic letter, immersed in the earthy realities of everyday Christian living: but the eschatological dimension is there right the way through, as the unstated but essential principle which undergirds the church's ongoing life (look back at 1:7–8; 3:13, 22; 4:5; 5:5; 6:1–2, 14; 9:24–27; 10:11). This is the hidden factor which relativizes individual concerns about marital status (7:26) or spiritual gifts (13:8–13). This is what binds together the community and motivates its religious practices (11:26; 15:29). Without it, the Christian's present life is as empty as the future (15:14–19), and Paul's missionary endeavours are completely pointless (15:30–32: 'wild beasts' here probably metaphorical, cf. 2 Corinthians 1:8–10).

6 Looking to the End   *Read 1 Corinthians 15:35–58*

It is hard to find anything to say about this chapter which is not better said (or sung!) in the passage itself. The coda to the letter (apart from the practical arrangements of chapter 16) is an extended, poetic meditation on the doctrine of resurrection in which Paul uses the diatribe style of philosophical debate (vv. 35–36) to expose the imaginative poverty of the sceptic's objections. The body, in Greek thought, was at best little more than a hindrance to the free and untrammelled activity of the soul: truth and beauty resided only in the eternal, heavenly realm. In insisting on the doctrine of the resurrection of the body, by contrast, Paul emphasized that we must take seriously both the heavenly and the earthly dimensions of human existence:

- *We must take seriously God's creative power (vv. 36–41). Looking at a gardener's autumn selection of seeds or bulbs would give a very limited idea of the variety and richness of the flowers of spring and summer: the one could not possibly be deduced from the other. C.S. Lewis compares our situation with that of a child, born and raised in a dungeon, trying to imagine the world of trees and mountains from pencil lines drawn on paper.*

- *We must take seriously the human condition (vv. 42–49). Death is an enemy to be defeated (vv. 26, 54–55). Bodies can be ridiculous and humiliating, all the more with the approach of age: they can be distorted by pain or torn apart in catastrophic accident. All these are things we can gladly discard, like the seed-husk as it decays into the ground. Even those who are alive at the time of the End will need to be 'changed' (vv. 50–53). What lies ahead is different beyond all our imaginings, as different as the sunflower from the seed or the butterfly from the caterpillar.*

- *We must take seriously the continuity: the unimaginable heavenly body is in some way the same person ('we') as the discarded earthly body. The body is not some arbitrarily chosen cipher for the soul. The two are biologically related: the sunflower is already there in the seed. And this means that the moral choices we make in this life do have eternal significance, just as Adam's did (v. 22). It was in the body that Christ won the victory over sin and death (vv. 55–57), and it is in the body that humanity is offered the choice of following him and sharing the same victory (vv. 20–23, 57).*

Far from encouraging an other-worldly downgrading of life 'in the body', then, the Christian doctrine of resurrection reinforces its eternal significance. The Christian cannot afford to divorce soul from body, as though what happens in the one has no effect on the other. It is in the body that holiness has to be put into practice, both at the individual level (6:13–14), and at the community level (11:29; 12:12–13). It is no coincidence that this letter which so dramatically concludes with the resurrection begins with the preaching of the cross (1:18ff.), the only basis for building something in this life which can survive the fire of judgment and last into the next (15:58, cf. 3:10–17).

Some starters for discussion and prayer:

- *On spiritual gifts: God 'wants to bring the man to a state of mind where he could design the best cathedral in the world, and know it to be the best, and rejoice in the fact, without being any more (or less) or otherwise glad at having done it than he would be if it had been done by another'* (C.S. Lewis, The Screwtape Letters).

- *On knowledge: 'The imperfection of our knowledge, even of revealed truth, is not sufficiently recognized; and hence the rejection of Christianity by so many thoughtful people. Christians often claim to know more than it is possible to know. They forget how much the Bible is symbolical'* (Robertson and Plummer).

- *On resurrection: 'Hasn't Easter got to be unexpected? not what we planned? The Jesus given back to the women and the other disciples is eventually recognizable, but not just the same. Jesus belongs with God now, so we meet Jesus in the way we meet God, someone who always goes beyond what we know and what we feel safe with. We can be frightened by this, we can be liberated by this—or both at once, most likely. And the church overall finds it so hard to believe that there can be a really new future that is really faithful to what has already been given. Yet that seems to be what the resurrection is'* (Rowan Williams, in Chrysalis: Women and Religion, Jan 1993).

- *On death: '"Flesh and blood," that is, the mere natural life, says St Paul, "cannot inherit the kingdom of God." To get to God they... have not merely to undergo death, they have to achieve death, have to make a positive use of death, to throw off their self-bound being so that God may receive a willing material for his own love to remake... There is no getting to God without passing through this fire, for, says Christ, "every man shall be salted with fire." The fire is salt, cleansing, healing, salutary, it is the fire of Christ's own sacrifice purifying us from self, making us fit for God, and in God for our true happiness. May God give me more of that holy fire here, so that I may not wait for another life before I begin to find and love and serve my only true good, my merciful creator. May God give me grace not to run from this fire, nor to throw away the cross'* (Austin Farrer, 'Nice and Worldly', in Said or Sung, Faith Press, 1964).

How deep I find your thoughts, O God: how great is the sum of them!
If I were to count them, they would be more in number than the sand;
to count them all, my lifespan would need to be like yours.
Search me, O God, and know my heart;
try me and know my restless thoughts.
Look well, and see whether there be any wickedness in me,
and lead me in the way that is everlasting.

from Psalm 139

For further reading

There has been a flood of serious studies of 1 Corinthians and its social world in recent years. These are just a selection.

Jerome Murphy-O'Connor, *St. Paul's Corinth: texts and archaeology*, Liturgical Press, Collegeville, Minn., 1990 gives a fascinating selection of first-century texts and documents relating to the city.

Gerd Theissen, *The Social Setting of Pauline Christianity*, T. & T. Clark, 1982 is a classic study and still in many ways the best introduction to the social issues in the letter.

Ben Witherington III, *Conflict and Community in Corinth*, Eerdmans/ Paternoster, 1995 gives a good recent wide-ranging entry into the debate (though it uses a rhetorical method to analyse the text which I have not followed in these notes).

I have quoted occasionally from A. Robertson and A. Plummer, *A Critical and Exegetical Commentary on the First Epistle of St. Paul to the Corinthians*, *The International Critical Commentary*, T. & T. Clark, 1911, which gives good old-fashioned exegetical notes on the Greek text.

For a more up-to-date commentary, Gordon D. Fee, *The First Epistle to the Corinthians*, *The New International Commentary on the New Testament*, Eerdmans, 1987 gives a good balanced approach.

For a really vigorous and lively insight into life in the Corinthian church (including some speculations on how the Corinthians might have answered back!) I would recommend Hans Frör, *You Wretched Corinthians!*, SCM Press, 1995.

Jonah

The book of Jonah is an outstanding illustration of the power of Old Testament storytelling. It is a gripping tale of times long past and customs strange, but its challenge is as fresh today as ever. And that challenge is multifaceted. The more scholars debate the meaning of the story, the more questions are raised and the more there is to discover of ourselves and of our God. For this is not a naïve story of extraordinary happenings appropriate to *The Guinness Book of Records*. That is not what the Bible is about, and not what God is about. It is deeply theological and as relevant in its challenge to us as it was to ancient Israel.

The only other reference to the prophet, and a brief one at that, is in 2 Kings 14:25. There his ministry is dated in the reign of Jeroboam II, roughly between 785 and 750BC. His message was an encouragement to the king in triumphantly restoring Israel's boundaries. Different though that is from the concerns of the book of Jonah, it provides something of a link, for Jonah's concerns were primarily with Israel, not with foreign nations, least of all with Nineveh, capital of Assyria which had been such a ruthless enemy to Israel.

The book of Jonah differs from the other prophetic books in that they give pride of place to the prophets' sayings rather than to narrative about the prophet. In this it is more akin to the stories of Elijah and Elisha, earlier prophets of the ninth century BC.

The notes are based, with some exceptions, on the NRSV.

16–22 FEBRUARY

1 Running from God *Read Jonah 1:1–10*

The book begins in a traditional way, precisely like the call which came to Elijah (1 Kings 17:8). But there the similarity ends, for 'Elijah set out and went...' Jonah's story immediately takes a surprising turn. God says, 'Arise and go'; Jonah 'arose to flee'. God says, 'Go east' (north-east to be precise); Jonah goes west!

This is a sophisticated, powerful narrative, yet with a grand simplicity more apparent in the original than it is in our modern idiomatic English translations where some of the significant repetitions of the Hebrew are lost. God said, 'Arise', but Jonah went down—down to

Joppa, down into the boat (v. 3), down into the hold of the ship (v. 5). Jonah thought himself a free agent, free to choose his own way against God's way. But there was another actor in the drama with whom Jonah had not reckoned. Jonah was fleeing from the presence of the Lord, so ends verse 3. Verse 4 begins with that same word, 'But the Lord...'

There is another striking repetition in chapter 1, more frequent even than the threefold 'he went down', and that is the word 'to hurl', variously translated in English. The Lord hurled a great wind on the sea. The sailors, afraid of shipwreck in the sudden ferocious storm, hurled the ship's cargo into the sea to lighten it. (For the other instances of 'hurl' see tomorrow's reading.) They, the Gentile sailors (Israel was not a seagoing nation), were busy working, busy praying. And Jonah, who had such freedom to choose that he could rebel against the Lord, was fast asleep below decks (v. 5). Jonah's freedom to choose proved to be only the freedom to opt out. God's purpose continued, but Jonah had sidelined himself. He becomes a passive figure in the story. Even the ship's captain had to waken him and urge him to pray.

See what Jonah answers to the sailors' questions. Identifying himself as a Hebrew, he makes a great confession of faith: 'I worship the Lord, the God of heaven, who made the sea and the dry land' (v. 9). And this is the God from whom he thinks he can flee—by sea! (Jonah had not learnt the truth of Psalm 139:7–10.) No wonder the sailors were frightened.

2 'Even the winds and the sea obey him' *Read Jonah 1:11–17*

Jonah at least was generous. Admitting that he was the cause of the problem, he suggests a drastic solution: 'Pick me up and hurl me into the sea.' The Gentile sailors come out of it well. They rowed hard to get back to land, reluctant to sacrifice a man's life and thus incur guilt themselves (v. 14). You may wish to read Psalm 107:23–30 for a vivid description of danger at sea, of prayer for deliverance, and of God's saving action for those 'at their wits' end' (v. 27 NRSV). And so, for the fourth time, we have that same word, 'they picked him up and hurled him into the sea'. But the Lord, the other actor in the drama, stepped in again. Jonah was to have a second chance, the chance to serve the Lord whom he had professed to worship: 'The Lord appointed a great fish...', and that verb, too, is repeated several times in the rest of the story. God was in control whatever Jonah might do. So there was Jonah 'in the belly of the fish' for three days and three nights, symbolic in the

New Testament of Jesus' death and resurrection (Matthew 12:40).

What Jonah had professed, and signally failed to do, namely to worship ('fear, reverence') the Lord, the sailors do. Having witnessed the Lord's control over the sea, both in destructive power and in calming the storm (cf. Jesus' action in Mark 4:41), they 'feared the Lord with a great fear' and offered a sacrifice. In other words 'they worshipped', and that not just for the moment but with vows, promises made for the future (v. 16).

3 Out of the depths! *Read Jonah 2:1–10*

By the beginning of chapter 2 not only has Jonah's situation changed, but his attitude, too, is transformed. For the first time in the story Jonah prays. Notice the significant words, 'to the Lord his God'. Jonah had turned his back on God, but now at last the relationship is re-established.

Jonah's psalm has much in common with psalms in the Psalter. The language used, of seas and drowning, suits Jonah's predicament up to a point, but not entirely, and the references to the temple (vv. 4 and 7), that is the Jerusalem temple, do not fit well with a prophet of the northern kingdom. It is likely that the psalm already existed independently. Its language is the traditional imagery of the psalms to depict distress and danger of many kinds. Such is the usage, for example, of 'Sheol', the underworld (cf. Psalm 18:5) and the reference to 'waves and billows' (cf. Psalm 42:7). There are echoes of other parts of the Old Testament, too, in Jonah's prayer. The idea that God will hearken to prayer whenever someone in trouble prays, in however distant a place, is beautifully expressed in Solomon's famous prayer at the dedication of the Jerusalem temple (1 Kings 8, especially vv. 27–30 and 49–50).

Dramatically the psalm has an important role in delaying the action of the story, but more significantly, it is at this point that Jonah's passive role begins to change. By verse 9 he has reached the same level of response as the Gentile sailors at the end of chapter 1.

Finally Jonah gives thanks, not now pleading for deliverance but affirming God's power to save. And the Lord responds. Jonah is rescued, but his task remains to be done. What the sailors had tried in vain to achieve (1:13) God's word effects, and Jonah is saved. He is to have a second chance.

4 God changes his mind   *Read Jonah 3:1–10*

The cycle of call and response begins again, underlined by a reminder for Jonah of the divine authority behind his message, 'proclaim to Nineveh the proclamation which I am telling you' (v. 2). Jonah has the privilege of a second chance. But why had he been reluctant in the first place? Surely a message of doom on Israel's ruthless enemy (soon to destroy the northern kingdom in 722BC) would have seemed appropriate to a nationalistic prophet such as Jonah. But for Jonah the situation was more complicated than that. The clue lies in 4:2. Jonah knew that God was compassionate, that he could 'change his mind', that judgment was not his last word. The demonstration of Yahweh's omnipotence in Jonah's rescue had changed his refusal into compliance, his reluctance into obedience, but it had not solved the prophet's dilemma. For Jonah the authenticity of his call, his credentials as a prophet, depended on the fulfilment of his message (Deuteronomy 18:22). But what if God changed his mind and the word was not fulfilled?

There is an ironic extravagance here in the story—the massive size of Nineveh, the immediacy of the repentance, the extent of the display of mourning with even the animals included in the sackcloth and fasting. But it is deeply serious in its challenge. What of Israel in contrast, the home of God's prophets, and its persistent refusal to repent? What of the prophet himself, called and chosen, but reluctant to obey? And what of us? God's word (to a fish!) had been effective for Jonah, why not (through a prophet) for the Ninevites?

Verse 9 is significant. The Ninevites are perceptive. They recognize God's sovereign freedom, that repentance is not a means to manipulate God. There is no guarantee of an automatic response: 'God may relent.' And he did, but this meant the non-fulfilment of his word, exactly what Jonah had feared. With the end of chapter 3 Nineveh's story is completed, but not Jonah's. The whole of chapter 4 is focused on him.

5 Jonah's dilemma   *Read Jonah 4:1–4*

Were it not for this last chapter it would be easy to summarize the purpose of the book of Jonah as the story of a mission avoided and a mission accomplished, and the portrait of the prophet as symbolic of God's people, reluctant to obey, in contrast to a foreign nation responsive to God's word (see Jesus' words in Matthew 12:41–42). And this is indeed an aspect of its meaning. The whole of this last chapter, however, focuses on the person of the prophet himself, on his contradictory emotions, and on the condescension of God who patiently reasons with him. It demonstrates not only the fact of God's mercy but the justification for it by analogy with the prophet's own emotions.

Notice how sadly the chapter starts: 'This (i.e. Nineveh's *deliverance*) was very displeasing to Jonah, and he became angry.' A prophet, saved from the consequence of his own disobedience, angry that God had saved those who were ready to obey! Jonah speaks several times in the last chapter, in fact it is a conversation between Jonah and God. And each time Jonah speaks it is in angry frustration. Death is better than life is his constant refrain (vv. 3, 8, 9). The man who chose 'freedom', or rather what he mistook for freedom, instead of service, his own will instead of God's, finds himself choosing death rather than life, the ultimate negative to end his story—a sad illustration of Psalm 1 with its contrasting choices and their consequences.

6 God's visual aids *Read Jonah 4:5–11*

Jonah responds to God's question not by word but by action (v. 5). This, too, is an opting out. He detaches himself from the city, becomes merely an observer of its fate for which in isolation he waits and watches, concerned only with his own comfort, building a shelter to provide himself with shade. But God who had 'appointed' a great fish for Jonah's deliverance (1:17) was still in control. He 'appointed a climbing gourd' to 'grow up above Jonah's head to throw its shade over him and relieve his discomfort' (REB). And now for the first time in the story Jonah was happy, very happy (v. 6). But next day God 'appointed' a worm, and Jonah's treasured plant withered. And still God had not finished with his lesson for Jonah nor with his visual aids. When the sun rose God 'appointed' a scorching wind, the sirocco blowing from the desert, and Jonah in distress longed for death. He was angry with God for the loss of his shady plant, something ephemeral on which he had expended neither care nor effort.

In a few brief words God draws his lesson (vv. 10–11). What Jonah had left out of account was 'pity', the word which furnishes the theme of the final two verses of the book: 'you pitied the gourd... Should I not pity the great city, Nineveh, with all these people in their ignorance, and all these animals?' Jonah had been angry, angry at the city's *salvation*, and angry at the gourd's *destruction* because at last his heart had been touched and his pity aroused at the waste of it all. If Jonah could be moved to pity, how much more the Lord! Here is the barrenness of self-love contrasted with divine compassion.

GUIDELINES

Jonah's is a story of extremes, of hope and of despair, of second chances, and of angry self-interest. It is a warning of what happens when professed belief and practical commitment drift apart, when knowledge of God's will is not lived out in life.

'Great is thy faithfulness, O God my Father.'
How great is my faithfulness?

Lord, for your word, the word of life that fires us,
Speaks to our hearts and sets our souls ablaze,
Teaches and trains, rebukes us and inspires us,
Lord of the word, receive your people's praise.

Timothy Dudley-Smith

For further reading

R.B. Salters, *Jonah and Lamentations*, Old Testament Guides, Sheffield Academic Press, 1994. A brief introductory work.

J. Magonet, *Form and Meaning. Studies in Literary Techniques in the book of Jonah*, Frankfurt, 1976. A more detailed study.

Daniel 1—7

Daniel, a book of stories and dreams, is about God's people under pressure. It divides into two: the first part (chapters 1–6) is about loyal Jews in exile in Babylon, led by the wise Daniel, who resist assimilation, while proving useful to the head of the state and earning his respect. Three young men and Daniel will not compromise their adherence to the Jewish Law, which they call the 'Law of the God of Heaven'. They prefer to face death, and God vindicates them. Some of the best remembered and most well-loved stories in the Bible belong to this first section of the book: the burning fiery furnace, the lions' den, Belshazzar's feast and the writing on the wall. The second part of the book (chapters 7–12) consists of visions which Daniel has and interpretations of these visions (given by God himself or by an angelic interpreter). These dreams point to the final working-out of God's purpose in history and to the deliverance he will provide to all those who trust in him. These chapters are the earliest example of the genre known as 'apocalyptic', a word that comes from the Greek *apokalypto*, 'I unveil' or 'I unwrap', and refers to the character of the material. Faithful Jews in time of persecution were reassured by visions or dreams of the final triumph of those who resisted the fiercest of pressures to the bitter end. Apocalyptic material contains the revelation or 'unveiling' of all kinds of heavenly secrets.

Daniel in Hebrew folk tradition was a legendary wise man (compare Ezekiel 14:14, 20; 28:3). Although the setting of the stories is in the sixth century BC (between 586 and 538BC, the exile according to biblical history), powerful internal indicators confirm that the book in its final form was put together during the persecution of pious Jews by the Syrian Greek king Antiochus Epiphanes IV. In December 167BC Antiochus actually set up a statue of Olympian Zeus in the temple in Jerusalem, which the author of Daniel refers to as 'the abomination that makes desolate' (11:31; compare 9:27 and 12:11). The first part of the book (chapters 1–6) contains the tales of Daniel and his companions and is told in the third person, while the visions that follow in chapters 7–12 are mostly told by Daniel himself. The book is written in two languages. Chapters 1:1—2:4a are in Hebrew. The rest of chapter 2 through to chapter 7 is in Aramaic, while chapters 8–12 are in Hebrew. These two languages and the structure of the book suggest that Aramaic popular tales have been inserted in a background of visionary experience and interpretation, which was in Hebrew and reflected more recent concerns.

These notes are based on the New Revised Standard Version of the Bible.

---

23 FEBRUARY–1 MARCH   *DANIEL 1:1—3:30*

1   Strange food in a strange land   *Read Daniel 1*

We open with the capture of Jerusalem and the downfall of King Jehoiakim of Judah. The capture of Jerusalem, while Jehoiakim was king, is not confirmed by the classical account of Jerusalem's overthrow in 2 Kings 24. There the king in question is Jehoiakim's son, Jehoiakin, though the invading Babylonian king is Nebuchadnezzar in all accounts. What mattered to the author of Daniel, however, is that his hero lives in the time of the exile, and that Jerusalem was devastated and plundered. Notice the depositing of temple vessels from Jerusalem in a Babylonian temple (v. 2). The land of Shinar in verse 2 is an old name for Babylon (compare Genesis 11:2). In verses 3–7 some of the best young Jewish men receive a grounding in Babylonian wisdom. 'Chaldeans' in verse 4 refers to Babylonian wise men. This is one of the internal pointers to a date later than the exile of the sixth century BC for the book of Daniel, for in Daniel's own time the word had a racial/ethnic meaning unlike its use in this context. In verse 7 the favoured exiles are given Babylonian names and eat food from the king's own table, a sure sign of royal favour. But Daniel will not compromise over the eating of Gentile food (v. 8). So a contest is proposed for Daniel and his three companions (vv. 11–13), who fare better on a vegetarian diet and water during a ten-day period of trial than the other young men who eat the king's unclean meat and drink his wine (vv. 14–17).

Moreover Daniel and the young men are rewarded for their steadfastness in the gifts of wisdom God gives them (v. 20). The reference to Cyrus (v. 21), the Persian conqueror of Babylon who let the Jews return to their own land in 539BC, informs us that the hero of the book was alive and at court throughout the entire period of the exile from 586BC, when deportations of Jews to Babylon by Nebuchadnezzar began, to 538BC when the return of some of them, according to the edict of Cyrus, occurred.

2   The king dreams a dream   *Read Daniel 2:1–24*

This chapter demonstrates what has been underlined in the preceding chapter. God has given Daniel a particular expertise in the interpretation of dreams. Compare the Joseph story in Genesis where Joseph interprets Pharaoh's dreams, when his own wise men have been unable to do so (Genesis 41).

Nebuchadnezzar has a dream which troubles him. The reference to the 'second year' of the king's reign in verse 1 may be a note deliberately added to impress the reader with a historical reference point, as it is hard to harmonize with the three-year period of education undergone by Hananiah, Mishael and Azariah in 1:5 (compare also 1:18). Other commentators argue that chapter 2:1 is virtually a new beginning to the book of Daniel and that the editor makes no attempt to harmonize the two accounts.

Nebuchadnezzar summons the experts to explain his dream. From verse 4, when the Chaldeans make their response to the king, all that follows up to 7:28 is in Aramaic. The king will not even tell his wise men the details of the dream (vv. 5–6), but requires from them first the dream and then its interpretation. The word 'interpretation' in verse 5 occurs some thirty times in chapters 2–7. Together with the word 'secret' or 'mystery', a word which also occurs frequently, it provides a glimpse into the agenda of apocalyptic. The king threatens his experts with dismemberment (v. 5), a severe oriental punishment known to us from ancient Mesopotamian documents. Verse 13 shows that Daniel and his three companions are about to be executed along with the Chaldeans. Daniel asks the king for time (v. 16), tells the three to offer prayers to the 'God of heaven' (v. 18) for illumination, and God reveals the dream and interpretation to him in a 'vision of the night' (v. 19). Daniel now blesses the name of God in a wonderful and moving doxology (vv. 20–21). God alone knows times and seasons, and he alone gives the gift of wisdom to the wise (v. 21), causing things long hidden in darkness to come to the light. Daniel asks to be brought to the king after imploring the king's officials not to execute the wise men (v. 24).

3   A dream of four kingdoms   *Read Daniel 2:25–39*

Arioch, the king's executioner, who would have seen to Daniel's punishment (see vv. 13–16), now brings him before the king (v. 25). When asked if he can tell the king his dream and its interpretation, Daniel answers that no wise man can reveal the mystery to the king on his own, but that God in heaven has chosen to reveal the dream to him. He now relates to Nebuchadnezzar the dream and its interpretation.

The dream, Daniel says, concerns what will happen 'at the end of days'. The phrase used here in verse 28 stands for the end of an era or period. It may be the end of time itself in some contexts but not here. The dream which Nebuchadnezzar had when he was asleep (v. 28) discloses what will happen in the future ('hereafter', v. 29) and the 'end of days' will close off this particular period—in this instance, presumably, the reign of Nebuchadnezzar.

The king's dream is of a great statue (v. 31). Most statues known from the literature of the ancient world were of gods, but this one is of four world empires. Notice here that there is deliberate irony in the feet (partly of iron and partly of clay) being the weakest part of the statue. For all its might and magnificence the statue has 'feet of clay'. The statue is atomized, crushed into small pieces and blown away on the wind like chaff. Daniel maintains a tone of proper respect and punctilious courtesy in his address to the king. Verse 37 uses the Persian royal mode of address, 'king of kings', and states that God has given him control over nature.

The interpretation Daniel gives is that the four different metals in this apparently descending series (v. 39, 'another kingdom inferior to yours') represent four kingdoms (compare the four beasts representing the same four kingdoms in chapter 7 below). Daniel says to the king: 'You are the head of gold' (v. 38). Thus the kingdom of gold is to be Babylon, the kingdom of legendary power and brilliance. Daniel does not identify the next three régimes as represented by the silver, the bronze, and the iron parts of the statue. Scholars are in universal agreement that the four kingdoms represent the kingdoms of the Babylonians, the Medes, the Persians and the Greeks. Historically the Median 'kingdom' is a literary fiction but in 5:30 and 6:28 a clear distinction is made between the reigns of the Medes and the Persians (compare also Isaiah 21:2 which also speaks of Media as an independent state power). In point of fact the kingdom of Media does not exist. Median lands were swallowed up by the emergent Persian empire.

4   Daniel concludes his interpretation   *Read Daniel 2:40–49*

We have to look outside the book of Daniel to identify these four kingdoms. The reference to the mixed character of the fourth kingdom in verse 42 ('part iron and part clay' rendering it 'partly strong and partly brittle') is held to refer to the composite nature of the Greek régime and the division of the empire of Alexander the Great between two successive kingdoms, the Seleucids to the north and the Ptolemaic kingdom to the south (with iron representing the Seleucids and clay the Ptolemies). This also covers the reference to the iron and clay mingling with one another in marriage, but not holding together (v. 43), for intermarriage between members of these rival dynasties had not succeeded in promoting lasting or stable alliances. In 200BC, after the battle of Paneas, Palestine had left the Ptolemaic sphere of influence and had come under the sway of the Seleucids to the north, which led eventually to the attempt of the Seleucid monarch, Antiochus Epiphanes IV, to suppress many Jewish religious observances.

Although the four kingdoms of the dream are represented as if they were all there at one and the same time, a sequence and a succession is envisaged. This is underlined and made clear in verse 44 where the 'kingdom that shall never be destroyed' is mentioned and is said to stand for the 'stone... cut from the mountain' (v. 45). The surreal dream language of the stone points for its symbolic content to the kingdom of Israel, which comes last of all, and which is to stand for ever (v. 44).

Here therefore we read about the restoration of God's people to their homes, and the dominance of the nation of Israel. Indeed the 'great mountain' (see v. 35, above) will fill the whole earth. This is exactly how Mount Zion is described throughout the Old Testament (compare Isaiah 2:2–3; Ezekiel 17:23; Psalm 2:6; 48:2–3).

Nebuchadnezzar honours Daniel by making obeisance to him, and offering incense to him in extravagant oriental fashion, as someone who knows God's secrets and who is appointed by God to reveal the interpretation of mysteries (v. 47). Like Joseph in the earlier story from Genesis, Daniel is promoted (v. 48) and, at his request, the three young men with him (v. 49). His star is in the ascendant, but of course we know that that is not the end of all his trials.

5 Macnamara's band, and a statue *Read Daniel 3:1–15*

Chapter 3 introduces a further test and further pressure on the Jews in exile to assimilate and break their cherished commandments. This time Nebuchadnezzar (you would think he would have learned by now) has a grotesque statue of fabulous dimensions built—according to verse 1, 90 feet by 9 feet! The statue is built on the Dura plain in Babylon—

shades of the tower of Babel here (compare Genesis chapter 11).

This entire chapter is full of lists, which were adored by Israel and the whole of the ancient world. Verse 5 introduces us to a kind of Macnamara's band of ancient oriental instruments. The names here are Greek loan words and there is speculation over what some of them stand for. The 'entire musical ensemble' in verse 5 is a translation of the Aramaic *sumponyah*, which may mean 'bagpipe'. The king was especially harsh in his dealings with the dissident and the disobedient: so this terrifying and triumphant cacophony of sound and the threat of the white hot furnace are sufficient deterrents for the potentially dissident. When Macnamara's band breaks out, therefore, the representatives of 'all peoples, nations and languages' gathered there on the plain of Dura before that unspeakable statue came crashing down to their knees (v. 7).

Not so Shadrach, Meshach and Abednego (v. 12), who do not join in this idolatry. We may well ask what has become of Daniel. He is absent from this story, which causes scholars to wonder whether the tale had any place in the original Danielic book of stories and visions. Whatever the truth of this, it does show us that the three can stand on their own feet and make their resistance to the king's demands without the help or encouragement of Daniel, trusting (as they say when they are brought before Nebuchadnezzar) in the God whom they serve (v. 17 below). They strike out on their own, rather like Peter, James and John in the Acts of the Apostles.

6 The burning, fiery furnace   *Read Daniel 3:16–30*

The idea of the furnace is interesting. Because the king can see what is happening inside the furnace, we can assume a beehive-shaped structure, rather like a lime kiln, possibly brick-built, with an opening at the top into which the men were thrown, and a door lower down, or at the side, through which the king could see the three walking about unharmed with their strange companion.

Punishment by being roasted in an incinerator was not unknown in the times of the Maccabees, those Jews who resisted Antiochus, when the book of Daniel was thought to have been compiled. In the Second Book of Maccabees (which is a part of our Apocrypha) a renegade Jewish high priest called Menelaus is thrown into 'a tower... 50 cubits high, full of ashes' with 'a rim running around it which on all sides inclines precipitously into the ashes' (2 Maccabees 13:5). This happened in 165BC at Aleppo in Syria.

There is a vivid attention to detail in the description of the three men 'bound, still wearing... tunics... trousers... hats... and... other garments' (v. 21). This and the repetition (four times in all, verses 5, 7, 10 and 15) of the list of orchestral instruments is a pointer to the oral nature of the story. It is a tale that was told, and which calls out for many retellings.

Between verses 23 and 24 the Greek Bible inserts a lengthy portion, which depicts the three walking in the midst of the flames and praising God. We are given here the content of their praise, first a long prayer by Azariah/Abednego, and then a hymn of praise, that great ecological canticle we call the *Benedicite* ('O all ye works of the Lord bless ye the Lord'), which we sing at Morning Prayer. You can find this additional portion together with all those other parts in the Greek Bible in the Apocrypha.

The fourth unknown companion to the three who walk unharmed in the furnace has 'the appearance of a god'—literally, 'the son of the gods' (v. 25). We are talking of an angel here, as Nebuchadnezzar realizes later (v. 28). Shadrach, Meshach and Abednego are not just delivered *from* the fire, but *in* the fire. Remember that beautiful verse from Isaiah which is sung as a lovely modern hymn these days: 'When you walk through fire you shall not be burned, and the flame shall not consume you' (Isaiah 43:2).

The dramatic cry of Nebuchadnezzar in verse 26 reminds me of Jesus summoning Lazarus in John's Gospel (John 11:43). There is no doubt at all in the story about the miraculous deliverance of the three Jewish martyrs. Nebuchadnezzar has witnessed it. So have the officials who are assembled to see the execution. The result of the stand taken by the three confessors and their miraculous deliverance is that all restrictions are lifted on the practice of their faith. No one, on pain of dismemberment, must utter blasphemy 'against the God of Shadrach, Meshach and Abednego' (v. 29). The Babylonians learned that the God of these three Jewish resisters was able to 'deliver in this way' (v. 29). Like Joseph in the Genesis story, Shadrach, Meshach and Abednego are promoted. Did our author, one wonders, hope that Antiochus Epiphanes, the oppressor of the Jews at the time when the Daniel book was put together, would relent and realize the benefits in terms of the stability of the realm of a generous policy towards religious minorities?

GUIDELINES

'He's got the whole world in his hands.' Or has he? Daniel would say that he has, and that whatever trials beset the person of faith, he or she will be vindicated by God, and God remains sovereign. It is hard to see this in Rwanda, in the internecine struggle in Northern Ireland, in the killing fields of Bosnia.

We can find equivalents today of the basic stories of deliverance in these first chapters of Daniel. 'Signs of the times' are always around to move us, modern tales of dire warning that seem to echo Danielic themes, and turn those who use power for immoral ends pale. The writer of the book of Daniel is indeed like the person who prays with a Bible in one hand, and a newspaper in the other.

Reading Daniel we are encouraged that there is justice, God's justice, in the world, and it will triumph. 'Now have come the salvation and the power and the kingdom of our God, and the authority of his Messiah' (Revelation 12:10).

2–8 MARCH   DANIEL 4:1—6:28

1   Trees and werewolves   *Read Daniel 4:1–18*

The chapter begins with a flourish! Nebuchadnezzar is pleased with himself. God has blessed him by working for him signs and wonders and he praises him (vv. 1–3). But everything does not stay well. He goes on to tell the story of a dream and its momentous outcome (v. 5), after it has been interpreted by Daniel. The Chaldean interpreters are summoned as before, but when they fail in their efforts, Daniel is called in (v. 8). Note the description of Daniel as 'one who is endowed with a spirit of the holy gods' (v. 8).

The dream is about a great tree at the centre of the earth (v. 10). Its top reaches heaven, and animals and birds find rest in its wide, sweeping branches with their abundant shade (vv. 11–12). A 'holy watcher', that is an angel (compare the hymn 'Ye watchers and ye holy ones'), comes down from heaven and cries out: 'Cut down the tree and chop off its branches...' (v. 14). For the motif of a lofty tree being felled, and a comparison of this with the humbling of a proud sovereign, compare Ezekiel 17 (where the king of Judah is a fruitful tree until it is uprooted), and Ezekiel 28 (for the arrogant posturing of a proud being, before he falls). There are fables in which trees figure in several parts of the Old Testament (for example Judges 9:8–15; 2 Kings 14:9) and the mythology of a sacred tree at earth's centre, linking earth to heaven, and bringing life and fruitfulness to the world, is a motif constantly occurring in ancient Middle Eastern literature. Compare also the tree of life in the Garden of Eden in the Genesis story (Genesis 2:9) and the part this plays in the temptation story of Adam and Eve and the serpent.

Verses 15–18 apply the image of the stricken tree to an anonymous figure. After the detail about only the stump of the tree being left reinforced with 'a band of iron and bronze' (v. 15) this unknown figure is introduced. He is not to have a home but to share the lot of the wild beasts and the birds, 'bathed with the dew of heaven' (v. 15). Furthermore for seven years (v. 16, 'seven times') this unfortunate figure is to inhabit the mental world of an animal. Werewolves were known in Daniel's day! The 'watchers' who make this decree and ordain this severe sentence against the luckless man in the vision intend to make it known that 'all who live may know that the Most High is sovereign over the kingdom of mortals' (v. 17). These 'watchers' are God's wakeful, angelic messengers whose eyes rove over all the world, and they often feature in the Jewish literature between the Testaments. God can give kingship to anyone who wishes to have it even to the 'lowliest of human beings' (v. 17). He can also take it away again. As Mary's Magnificat says, 'He has put down the mighty from their seat and has exalted the humble and meek' (Luke 1:52). Compare also the Song of Hannah in 1 Samuel 2:7–8 and Psalm 113:7–8. Joseph is a classic instance of this rags to riches, 'log cabin to White House' kind of story.

The king now asks Daniel to interpret the dream where others had failed, ending with those significant words underlined on his *curriculum vitae* mentioned also in verse 8: '... for you are endowed with a spirit of the holy gods' (v. 18).

2 The wild man is restored to his kingdom   Read Daniel 4:19–37

Daniel is terrified at the thought of communicating to Nebuchadnezzar the dream and its interpretation. After an assurance from the king (v. 19), he begins explaining that the tree is the king. The pride of the king, which has grown too great, is to be brought low. In his exile Nebuchadnezzar is to learn that God rules, 'that the Most High has sovereignty over the kingdom of mortals, and gives it to whom he will' (v. 25). Not that Nebuchadnezzar's kingdom is to be taken away from him. The presence of the stump in the dream, reinforced by iron and bronze, is itself a sign that the king will be restored to his kingdom 'from the time that you learn that Heaven is sovereign' (v. 26). This is the only time in the whole Old Testament where 'heaven' is used for God, although the use of it does gain ground by the time of Jesus (compare Luke 15:18, 21).

Daniel now calls on the king to atone for his sins by practising almsgiving. This is the technical meaning of 'righteousness' (v. 27). Nebuchadnezzar is given a year to repent. When he was walking on his palace roof, extolling the magnificence he could see around him, which, he said, 'I have built... by my mighty power and for my glorious majesty' (v. 30), a heavenly voice came and pronounced sentence against him (v. 31). The detail of the voice from heaven is reminiscent of an expression often found in rabbinic literature, 'the daughter of a voice', meaning a voice from heaven or a mysterious supernatural voice. Compare the 'still small voice' of 1 Kings 19:12, or the voice heard at the baptism of Jesus (Matthew 3:17; Mark 1:11; Luke 3:22). Verse 33 tells us that Nebuchadnezzar was immediately driven away from human society and began to live like an animal. He became a wild Neanderthal, or werewolf-like creature (v. 33). At the end of a whole year, like the Ancient Mariner in Coleridge's poem, Nebuchadnezzar lifts his eyes to heaven and repents, and his reason is restored. He praises God and acknowledges his sovereignty (vv. 34 and 35) and he receives back all the majesty and glory he once had (v. 36). Nebuchadnezzar ends by praising and extolling 'the King of heaven' (v. 37). This phrase, only found here in the Old Testament, emphasizes that God is the only sovereign.

It must be said that we have no record of Nebuchadnezzar suffering a severe nervous attack like the one here depicted. It is suggested Nebuchadnezzar's madness contains a covert allusion to Nabonidus, the last Babylonian king, who retired to the faraway oasis of Teima when his empire was seriously threatened. That the reference in this chapter is to Nabonidus rather than to Nebuchadnezzar has support from a manuscript called the *Prayer of Nabonidus* among the Dead Sea Scrolls found at Qumran. (See G. Vermes, *The Dead Sea Scrolls in English*, fourth edition, Penguin, 1995, page 329.)

3 Belshazzar's feast   *Read Daniel 5:1–23*

This is one of the most well-known and colourful passages in the book of Daniel. Artists love to paint this creepy and atmospheric story of the feast and the writing on the wall. King Belshazzar, although portrayed here as being the son and successor of Nebuchadnezzar, was in fact the son of the last Babylonian king Nabonidus (555–538BC). It was in his reign that the proud Babylonian empire fell to the army of the Persian king Cyrus. When Nabonidus spent the last part of his unhappy reign in the oasis of Teima, affairs were placed in the hands of his son Belshazzar, who was never recognized as king. The use of the sacred vessels looted from the Jerusalem temple by 'the king, his lords, his wives and his concubines', would have been a reminder of the more recent plunder of the temple, especially by Antiochus Epiphanes (compare 2 Maccabees 5:15ff).

There exists a Babylonian document scholars call the *Nabonidus Chronicle* which tells of a great feast to celebrate the Babylonian new year, held in the year that Babylon fell. A lot of wine was drunk at this feast and the cult connected with the festival included the worship of a large number of local deities. Verse 4 is entirely congruent with this historical background. As soon as this sacrilege was committed a hand appeared and wrote a message of dire importance on the wall, 'next to the lampstand' (v. 5), where the king could see it. Belshazzar nearly collapses with fear and proclaims that the one from his troupe of Chaldeans and wise men who can read the writing on the wall will be suitably honoured and rewarded. None of the official wise men can make sense of the writing. Daniel is therefore sent for at the instigation of the queen. The king promises him the honours already on offer to the one who can interpret the writing but Daniel, knowing the menace and warning embodied in the writing, refuses all rewards. 'Nevertheless,' he says, 'I will read the writing to the king and let him know the interpretation' (v. 17).

Daniel prefaces his warning by recalling the fate of Nebuchadnezzar (v. 21). Nebuchadnezzar learned his lesson, but his experiences (Nebuchadnezzar is called Belshazzar's father in verse 18) have not influenced Belshazzar, who desecrated the temple vessels by drinking from them in this orgiastic feast. The 'gods of silver and gold' have been honoured, but 'the God in whose power is your very breath, and to whom belong all your ways, you have not honoured' (v. 23).

Such a passage with its terrific warning against despoilers of the temple, those who desecrate its property and defile its holy objects, would have provided a powerful encouragement to those who looked on at the doings of Antiochus Epiphanes or those who came earlier.

4 Weighed and found wanting *Read Daniel 5:24–31*

Daniel now reads the writing. There is no doubt that it is possible to interpret each of its words in a number of different ways, and scholarly commentators have had a field day doing this. A consensus, however, does emerge among the plethora of interpretations. Daniel reads the words, and then gives the interpretation. 'MENE' equals a 'mina' (a weight of 500 or 600 grams). It is repeated, either for emphasis, as it is the first in the series of three, or through a scribal error (what is called dittography, which means writing a word or phrase twice). 'TEKEL' equals 'shekel' (a weight of ten grams). 'PARSIN' equals a 'half-shekel' (or rather 'half-shekels', the plural of PERES in verse 28). The whole inscription, therefore, as read out by Daniel, is a bit like a trader's call in a commercial centre: 'It's worth a mina, a shekel and [two] halves.' This is obviously a series descending in value. A 'mina' is worth more than a 'shekel', a 'shekel' more than a 'peres' and so on. Some scholars say that named or actual Babylonian kings underlie these weights. Other commentators argue that the weights are an indication of what the kingdom used to be worth, and what it is now worth, or shortly will be worth. The kingdom will fall into two halves (the verb *peras* means 'to break in half'), divided between two rulers, possibly between Median and Persian kings. And of course 'PARSIN' is a pun on the Persians who under Cyrus will eventually come to possess the entire kingdom.

Having given the overt 'meaning' of the words, Daniel goes on to give the covert, or allegorical meaning. The words are used for weights precisely because they stand variously for the activities of counting, measuring, or weighing, or dividing up. So:

- *the Aramaic verb* menah, *underlying MENE, is used commonly to mean 'to count'. Hence 'God has numbered the days of your kingdom and brought it to an end' (v. 26).*

- *the verb* tekal *underlying TEKEL means 'to weigh a person's moral value or worth in a balance or scales'. Hence '... you have been weighed on the scales and found wanting' (v. 27). And...*

- *the verb* peras *underlying PERES means 'to break in half', and the noun* paras *means Persia. Hence '... your kingdom is divided and given to the Medes and the Persians' (v. 28).*

Imagine if our word Persia had the connotation of 'being broken', and we heard Daniel interpret it thus: 'Your kingdom will be

Persianized.' Compare the verb to 'Balkanize', meaning to 'split into small pieces', as frequently happened in the politics of Balkan states.

Despite Daniel's earlier refusal (v. 17) he is nevertheless honoured, and 'that very night' Belshazzar is killed and Darius the Mede 'received the kingdom' (v. 30–31). We do not know in history of any 'Darius the Mede' succeeding by violence Nabonidus and his regent son Belshazzar. History rather shows that Cyrus the Persian took the city of Babylon by a kind of bloodless coup. There are overtones and hints of the death of the last Babylonian king in some Greek sources. Xenophon, the classical Greek historian, states that the Persian conquerors killed the Babylonian king, who was noted for his godlessness and cruelty (see Xenophon, *Education of Cyrus*, chapters 4–7).

Whatever the reality of the event in history, what we have here in Belshazzar's sudden and violent death is an extraordinary and totally unexpected calamity which was responsible for the overthrow of the kingdom and for the death of a man whom God was punishing (in the terms of the writing on the wall) for his sacrilege.

5 Daniel in the lions' den   *Read Daniel 6:1–15*

This well-known and colourful chapter is about the victory of prayer and of the faithful person who perseveres in prayer. Daniel is now serving the Persian king Darius, who established 120 satrapies (provinces with their governors). The figure may be a rhetorical exaggeration but the important thing is that Daniel is made one of the three most powerful men in the Persian empire (compare verse 29 in the previous chapter, where it is proclaimed of Daniel that 'he should rank third in the kingdom'). The satraps are responsible to three 'presidents', among whom Daniel is included, and the presidents ensure 'that the king might suffer no loss' (v. 2) and that the correct amount of revenue comes in.

Out of sheer jealousy a conspiracy is hatched by the remaining two presidents, and by the satraps, to find cause for complaint against Daniel. However, no corruption or negligence can be levied against him (v. 4). They look, therefore, to Daniel's loyalty to God and to his devotion to 'the law of his God' (v. 5), tricking the king into signing a decree that anyone who 'prays to anyone, divine or human, for thirty days, except to you, O king, shall be thrown into a den of lions' (v. 7).

The king is in a dilemma. Did he not foresee that Daniel would be the target for his officials, the reason for the decree? Obviously not. The officials are unanimous that the decree should be passed. It would reinforce the king's divine honours, and act as a means of obtaining the loyalty of his subjects. To Daniel, by contrast, and his enemies know this, the decree announcing that the king must be worshipped threatens his acknowledgment of the true God. In verse 8 we have the celebrated remark about 'the law of the Medes and the Persians which cannot be revoked'. There is nothing in history which supports the gullibility of the king in this context and against this background, although the idea of the king's irrevocable decree does receive some support from the book of Esther. In Esther 8:8 it is stated that 'an edict written in the name of the king and sealed with the king's ring cannot be revoked'. The suggestion is here that Persian law was stricter than the law had been under the Babylonians.

Whatever the support for it in history or otherwise, the idea of the irrevocable law provides a good story, one which teaches the virtue of faithful prayer, and brave and flawless steadfastness in the practice of the Jewish religion. 'How could we sing the Lord's song in a foreign land?' asks the psalmist (Psalm 137:4), and the answer is 'Dare to be a Daniel', as the opening line of a popular Sunday school chorus has it.

Daniel continues to pray three times a day despite the decree (v. 10). The psalmist prays three times a day (compare Psalm 55:17). Rabbinic Judaism prescribes morning, afternoon and evening as times for prayer, and the example of Daniel is cited, with the comment that, as Daniel did this, the practice must have arisen before the exile started. During one of the three times of prayer the conspirators discover Daniel and report him to the king. They do not, however, point to him directly but ask the king whether the decree still stands (v. 12). When the king agrees, they tell him that, despite the decree, Daniel is saying his prayers three times a day.

6 'You will tread on the lion and the adder' (Psalm 91:13)
Read Daniel 6:16–28

Despite the king's evident distress (v. 14), he holds fast to his edict (v. 16). Daniel is thrown into the lions' den. The king seals the mouth of the cave with his own signet (vv. 16 and 17), and has no sleep that night for thinking about Daniel (v. 18). At daybreak the king hurries to the den. Notice how he addresses Daniel ('Servant of the living God', v. 20) with an expression which to an Israelite is very expressive of a courageous faith (compare Deuteronomy 5:26; Psalm 42:2). Daniel emerges with the stunning declaration that 'God sent his angel and shut the lions' mouths' (v. 22). Did the lions leave Daniel untouched because they had been fed during the day, as Josephus the Jewish historian of the first Christian century wondered? We are not supposed to speculate rationally on this or to express moral indignation at the fate of the conspirators and their wives and children (v. 24). Collective punishment was an ancient practice (compare Joshua 7:24ff; 2 Samuel 21:5–9), although Jeremiah (31:29ff) and Ezekiel (chapter 18) criticize the injustice of it.

Daniel's God is now to be recognized, and the king praises this God who 'works signs and wonders in heaven and on earth, for he has saved Daniel from the power of the lions' (v. 27). Daniel continues, therefore, to prosper (v. 28). The trust he displays becomes proverbial in Jewish tradition. Compare the anonymous reference to him in the Epistle to the Hebrews where the writer mentions among the great heroes of the faith 'those who through faith conquered kingdoms, ministered justice, obtained promises, shut the mouths of lions, quenched raging fire, escaped the edge of the sword...' (Hebrews 11:33–34).

GUIDELINES

Do we fear God? Daniel was fearful of the encounter with God in his visions and times of prayer. Old hymns and liturgies speak of fearing God. Perhaps the expression should be shifted to the sense of *honouring* God, like those Gentile sympathizers with Judaism in New Testament times called 'God fearers' (compare Acts 13:43; 18:7). Daniel and his friends in exile honour God, and keep their covenant with him. They do not compromise, whether threatened with lions, or with beasts of nameless horror.

The seventeenth-century Bedfordshire tinker, John Bunyan, who wrote in his imprisonment a very Danielic book, *The Pilgrim's Progress*, was a man who could not and would not compromise. His faith in Christ was as strong as Daniel's faith in the Most High God, strong as the faith of those members of the young Church who did not compromise when persecution came.

We close this week with Bunyan's Pilgrim's hymn, perhaps one of the classic hymns for Christians under pressure. Bunyan's allegory of the Christian's journey through life, and the book of Daniel, which can be read as an allegory of the trials that beset us, are good resources to take with us on our way through Lent, and indeed through life.

Who would true valour see,
Let him come hither;
One here will constant be,
Come wind, come weather;
There's no discouragement
Shall make him once relent
His first avowed intent
To be a pilgrim.

Whoso beset him round
With dismal stories,
Do but themselves confound;
His strength the more is.
No lion can him fright;
He'll with a giant fight,
But he will have the right
To be a pilgrim.

No goblin nor foul fiend
Can daunt his spirit;
He knows he at the end
Shall life inherit.
Then, fancies fly away;
He'll not fear what men say;
He'll labour night and day
To be a pilgrim.

9–15 MARCH   DANIEL 7:1–28

1 Monsters from the deep *Read Daniel 7:1–4*

A new section of the book begins with this chapter. Chapters 7–12 are
a series of dream visions in which Daniel is the dreamer and God, or
an angelic interpreter, makes the vision plain to him. These chapters are
a 'book of dreams', like one of the long continuous sections of the book
of Enoch, a big and popular book contemporary with Daniel, but outside the biblical canon (cf. Genesis 5:24), in which the antediluvian
character Enoch, gifted as a seer and commissioned as a messenger
from God, receives news in a series of heavenly visions of what is to
come on the stage of world history. This is precisely what happens to

Daniel in the second part of the book that bears his name. Moreover we are placed for the purposes of this part of the book in a new time scale and time reference. Whereas chapter 6 finished with an event in the time of Darius (Belshazzar's successor), we now go back in time to the start of the reign of Nabonidus and his regent Belshazzar (v. 1—'in the first year of King Belshazzar of Babylon'). The vision develops by making predictions of things that are going to happen in the time of the Maccabees, and makes reference to the doings of Antiochus Epiphanes, the Syrian/Greek king who persecuted the Jews in the 160s BC.

Daniel dreams at night and writes down his dreams. In the dream winds from the four corners of heaven lash at the sea and stir it up and four great beasts emerge from the watery chaos (v. 3): a lion, a bear, a leopard and an undefined monster with ten horns (vv. 4–7). In the code language of Jewish apocalyptic, where dreams and interpretations figure frequently, angelic figures are represented by men (compare below 7:13), while human figures, especially kings of Gentile nations, are represented by animals (see Margaret Barker, *The Lost Prophet*, SPCK, 1988, page 27). The four beasts stand for the same four world empires as the four metals in chapter 2 above. The first beast, 'like a lion with eagle's wings', thus represents Babylon. The plucking off of the creature's wings, and its acquisition of a human mind symbolizing transformation from beast to man, and a human posture, is a sign of God's favour (v. 4). The lion-eagle, the Babylonian empire, becomes humanized.

2 The bear, the leopard, and the unnamed beast
Read Daniel 7:5–8

The second beast, standing for the Median empire, is 'like a bear'. The bear is half crouching and its mouth is crammed (v. 5) with tusks and teeth. Unlike Babylon it has no alleviating features, and the savagery of this fictitious kingdom of Media is echoed both by this description, and in the references in the Prophets to the Medes and the kings of the Medes (e.g. Isaiah 13:17ff; Jeremiah 51:11, 28). In actual fact, the Medes, who came from the Iranian plateau, fought with, mixed with, and ultimately went to make up the Persian nation.

The third beast, a leopard, is the kingdom of Persia (v. 6). But like the other beasts it is no ordinary example of the species. In apocalyptic dream imagery many beasts who represent kings or particular individuals are heraldic beasts, with hybrid features. So the leopard has four wings and four heads.

The fourth beast (v. 7), which symbolizes the Greek kingdom, is too terrible to be named. There is deadly menace in its description ('it had great iron teeth and was devouring, breaking in pieces...' v. 7), in being singled out as the epitome of terror and strangeness ('it was different from all the beasts that preceded it'—v. 7). Scholars have identified this beast's ten horns with the ten kings mentioned in apocalyptic literature outside Daniel who reigned throughout the period of the four empires. Alternatively ten could simply be a number suggesting several, although the detail that the little horn of verse 8 springs up and uproots three of the beast's ten horns might mean that the number ten is indeed significant, and that the reference is to Antiochus Epiphanes brushing aside the men in order to gain the throne. Antiochus is the horn that has the 'mouth speaking arrogantly' which is expanded into a statement of his aggressive impieties in verse 25 below.

The scene now switches to the heavens where God sits with his heavenly council in judgment. For the common idea of God and his council compare 1 Kings 22:19ff, Job 1:6ff, Isaiah 6:6ff and Psalm 89:7.

3 The Ancient One takes his throne *Read Daniel 7:9–12*

The stage is set for the overthrow of the four beasts: 'As I watched thrones were set in place and an Ancient One took his throne...' (v. 9). Verses 9 and 10 burst into poetry to describe the enthronement of this 'Ancient One'. Of course this Ancient One is God, although he is not described like this anywhere else in the Old Testament. The word 'Ancient One', as it is translated in the New Revised Standard Version, has an Aramaic expression underlying it which the Authorized Version, the Revised Version and the Revised Standard Version translate as 'the Ancient of days' or 'one that was ancient of days'. The idea is that God existed from eternity (compare Isaiah 44:6). There is a similar description of the Canaanite God El in the texts from Ras Shamra, Ancient Ugarit, in Syria.

We have here in this passage with its description of God on his throne, with myriad upon myriad of attendant angels, a classic example of what scholars and commentators call a 'throne vision', that is, a vision of God on his throne surrounded by his heavenly council, with the throne wreathed in fire. The context of the visions is almost always a judgment scene (compare 1 Kings 22:19–22, Isaiah 6 and, though there are some differences here, Ezekiel chapter 1, which has influenced this chapter of Daniel very greatly). A seminal influence on this throne passage in the book of Daniel is also the book of Enoch, a work which was very important to the Jews of Daniel's time, and has been alluded to earlier in this section of notes. In the first of the five 'Enoch' books which make up the whole book of Enoch, there is a passage in which Enoch is called up into the heavenly world and approaches God's throne. Daniel 7, while developing differently, is heavily indebted to this passage. (See 1 Enoch 14 in J.H. Charlesworth, *The Old Testament Pseudepigrapha*, volume I, Darton, Longman and Todd, 1983, pages 20–21.)

Verses 10 and 11 depict the heavenly court in session. Sentence is pronounced against the fourth beast, the one whose arrogance has already been noted, and it is put to death with its body consigned to the flames. 'Hellfire becomes the standard place and mode of eschatological punishment from this time on; compare the lake of fire in Revelation 20:10' (John J. Collins, *Daniel. A Commentary on the book of Daniel*, Minneapolis, 1993, page 304).

The other three beasts meanwhile have their power taken away, but their lives are spared 'for a season and a time' (v. 12). Throughout the Greek age in Jewish Palestine and beyond into Roman times, traces of independent Median and Persian principalities remain, all historical anachronisms, with none of their old sovereignty, power or prestige.

4   Like a son of man   *Read Daniel 7:13–18*

A manlike figure now comes with the clouds of heaven before the Ancient One, there to be given 'dominion and glory and kingship' (vv. 13–14). 'Scarcely any passage in the Hebrew Bible has engendered as much controversy as this phrase.' Collins in his commentary on Daniel (page 304) is of course referring to the description of the second figure in verse 13, 'one like a human being', or 'one like a son of man', as the underlying Aramaic has been rendered in earlier translations.

'The clouds of heaven' identify the manlike figure as a heavenly figure, and some scholars, on the analogy of the descriptions of the archangel Gabriel in Daniel 8:15–17; 9:21; 10:5, or of Michael, 'the great prince, the protector of your people' in 12:1, argue that the figure is to be identified with one of these archangels. The explanation of the dream, when Daniel asks one of the attendant angels, is that the four beasts are four kings, but the 'holy ones of the Most High' shall possess the kingdom for ever (vv. 15–18). So the manlike figure, others argue, could be the personification of these 'holy ones' in verse

18. Four beasts stand for four kings, one like a son of man personifies and stands for holy ones. It is also noteworthy that the one like a son of man is intended to contrast dramatically with the four savage beasts. They stand for terror and bestial savagery, the manlike figure for rescue and peaceful and humane sovereignty.

For the most part, however, 'holy ones' is used of angelic beings (like the word 'man' in Jewish apocalyptic literature). That is how it is used in the literature of the Dead Sea Scrolls. It is used also, however, of those who aspire to the status of the angels, because of their outstanding piety and fidelity and pureness of living. So 'holy ones' here in Daniel (7:18) could mean angelic or heavenly beings, and the 'people of the holy ones of the Most High' in verse 27 below could refer to those faithful Israelites whose steadfastness in times of persecution are noted by God, and who (to coin a phrase from the Qumran Hymns) are enabled to 'stand with the host of the Holy Ones', and 'enter into community with the congregation of the Sons of Heaven' (see G. Vermes, *The Dead Sea Scrolls in English*, 4th Edition, Penguin, 1995, page 198).

In some rabbinic passages the 'one like a son of man' has a messianic connotation, while the figure in Revelation 1:12ff. partakes of the characteristics of both figures in Daniel 7, the Ancient One and the manlike figure, and so is undoubtedly God in Christ. Certainly Christian tradition has tended to see in Daniel 7:13 the figure of Christ, who comes to judge the world, and who is given 'the victory'.

In our Daniel passage victory comes to the 'one like a human being', and he is invested in his appearance before God, the Ancient One, with sovereignty (v. 14). This investiture has overtones of the same traditions we encounter in the so-called 'royal psalms'. In Psalms 2, 89 and 110 the coronation of God's anointed one is associated with both his victory over his enemies and his prosperous and peaceful rule as God's vice-regent.

5 The truth about the fourth beast   *Read Daniel 7:19–22*

The interpretation of the fourth beast (vv. 19–20) makes clear to Daniel and to the readers what kind of adversary the 'holy ones of the Most High' are dealing with. In verse 21 the little horn, Antiochus Epiphanes, makes war on the holy ones. In verse 25 it is said that he 'shall speak words against the Most High', doubtless an allusion to the fact that Antiochus was the first Hellenistic ruler to add the words 'God Manifest' on his coins, a particularly blasphemous thing to do in the eyes of faithful Jews. For an ancient and near-contemporary account of Antiochus' depredations against the Jews of Jerusalem, see 1 Maccabees 1:29–40.

The decree of Antiochus, 'that all should be one people' throughout his empire, and the effect this is to have on observant Jews, follows in 1 Maccabees 1:41ff. The allusions in verse 25, 'he shall attempt to change the sacred seasons and the law' is in line with what is stated in 1 Maccabees 1:44–45:

> And the king sent letters by messengers to Jerusalem and the towns of Judah; he directed them to follow customs strange to the land, to forbid burnt offerings and sacrifices and drink offerings in the sanctuary, to profane sabbaths and festivals...

The reference in the second part of verse 25, '... and they shall be given into his power for a time, two times, and half a time', is to three and a half years. The Aramaic word for 'time' is understood as a 'year'; hence 'a year, (two) years and half a year'. To some commentators this is therefore an accurate prediction of the time (three years from December 167BC to December 164BC) during which the Jerusalem temple had been in a state of defilement. Compare echoes of this terrible period of defilement in Revelation 11:2, 'and they will trample over the holy city for forty-two months'. For others three and a half years is simply a round number, like half a dozen, and no exactness of description is intended.

6 The fall of the fourth beast, and the victory of the holy ones
Read Daniel 7:23–28

Finally judgment is pronounced against the little horn, and the kingdom given to 'the people of the holy ones of the Most High' (vv. 26–27). Daniel is terrified, and ponders long and hard on what he has seen and learned (v. 28). Compare here the penultimate verse of the famous nativity chapter in St Luke's Gospel: 'His mother treasured all these things in her heart' (Luke 2:51).

Chapter 7 anticipates what is worked out in detail in the remaining chapters: that the victory of the people of God in this cosmic conflict is assured. Made clear in a vision rich in animal symbolism in chapter 8 (with details of it interpreted by the angel Gabriel), this triumph is never in doubt.

Daniel, however, is eager to discover the full outworking of the vision in detail. He repents on behalf of his nation in sackcloth and ashes in chapter 9, and sees a heavenly being in chapter 10, together with other angels who inform him what is to take place among all the Hellenistic kingdoms until the time of Antiochus and his sacrilege (chapter 11), predicting the end of Antiochus (11:45), and the final vindication, when Michael will do battle as angel champion of Israel (12:1). 'Everlasting life' will come to the faithful in a general resurrection from 'the dust of the earth', 'everlasting contempt' to the others (12:2).

Our writer says nothing of any historical validity about how Antiochus Epiphanes really died, nor does he ever allude to the rededication of the temple in Jerusalem in 164BC. Instead, he writes before these things took place, with hope in his heart, on the eve of the end of days, and seals up his book 'until the time of the end' (12:9, 13).

GUIDELINES

We are never alone. God's messengers are everywhere. Daniel saw them in his visions or heard them speaking to him (in chapters 4, 7, 8 and 10), and our worship in church calls upon 'angels and archangels, and the whole company of heaven' at our service of holy communion.

William Blake, the mystical English poet, artist and engraver, wrote: 'What, it will be questioned, when the sun rises, do you not see a round disc of fire somewhat like a guinea? Oh no, no, I see an innumerable company of the heavenly host crying Holy, Holy, Holy is the Lord God Almighty.'

Daniel's book is about heavenly beings and their dealings with human beings. To his visionary eye angels lurk in all places. Perhaps, after reading the book of Daniel, we should open our eyes a bit more, like Elisha encouraged his young companion to do in another biblical story, when he could not see the heavenly host who had come down to protect them both:

> When an attendant of the man of God rose early in the morning and went out, an army with horses and chariots was all around the city. His servant said, 'Alas, master! What shall we do?' He replied, 'Do not be afraid, for there are more with us than there are with them.' Then Elisha prayed: 'O Lord, please open his eyes that he may see.' So the Lord opened the eyes of the servant, and he saw; the mountain was full of horses and chariots of fire all around Elisha.

> 2 Kings 6:15–17

103

In Daniel 7:10 angels are at hand for the judgment scene. I leave you with some words from a poem by the famous padre of the Great War, Geoffrey Anketell Studdert-Kennedy, nicknamed Woodbine Willy, based on Daniel 7 and on the parable of the sheep and goats in Matthew 25:31–46:

> *Our padre were a solemn bloke,*
> *We called 'im dismal Jim.*
> *It fairly gave ye t' blooming creeps*
> *to sit and 'ark at 'im,*
> *When 'e were on wi' Judgement Day,*
> *Abaht that great white throne,*
> *And 'ow each chap would 'ave to stand*
> *And answer on 'is own.*
> *And if 'e tried to chance 'is arm,*
> *And 'ide a single sin,*
> *There'd be the angel Gabriel,*
> *Wi' books to do 'im in.*

'Seal the books until the end', the angel says to Daniel. To the modern reader I say, looking wistfully at Woodbine Willy's verse, epitome of our violent, Danielic century: 'Don't let the books do you in.'

For further reading

Margaret Barker, *The Lost Prophet*, SPCK, 1988

J.H. Charlesworth, *The Old Testament Pseudepigrapha*, volume I, Darton, Longman and Todd, 1983

John J. Collins, *Daniel. A Commentary on the Book of Daniel*, Fortress Press, Minneapolis, 1993

P.R. Davies, *Daniel*, Sheffield Academic Press, 1993

John E. Goldingay, *Daniel*, Word Biblical Commentary, volume 30, Dallas, Texas, 1989

E.W. Heaton, *The Book of Daniel*, Torch Commentary, SCM Press, 1956

D.S. Russell, *Divine Disclosure*, SCM Press, 1992

Geza Vermes, *The Dead Sea Scrolls in English*, 4th edition, Penguin, 1995

Mark 9:30—16:8

Our earlier readings in Mark's Gospel brought us to the point at which Jesus asked his disciples who they thought he was. His response to Peter's bold 'you are the Christ' filled them with confusion and horror. He announced his intention to go to Jerusalem, not as the leader of an army of liberation, but to face rejection, suffering and death from the leaders of his own people. If the disciples wanted confirmation of the rightness of Jesus' grasp of his destiny, three of them were offered a glimpse of the glory of Jesus on the mountain of transfiguration. There they heard the voice of God, urging them to listen to his Son. Meanwhile the other nine were failing in their attempts to rid a young boy of a dumb and destructive spirit.

As we shall see, the disciples' struggle to share the faith of Jesus continues as they make their way from Galilee to Jerusalem.

16–22 MARCH   **MARK 9:30—10:45**

1   Passion predictions   *Read Mark 9:30–32*

These verses contain the second of three predictions relating to Jesus' fate (cf. 8:31; 10:32–34). The structure of each is similar, with Jesus referring to himself as the Son of Man and describing how he is to be handed over to face suffering and death before rising again on the third day. Characteristically, each one results in misunderstanding or incomprehension on the part of the disciples.

It seems unlikely that Jesus could foresee his fate in such detail, not least because the certainty of resurrection reflected in these verses is at variance with the anguish he suffered in Gethsemane and on the cross (all this becomes rather hollow if Jesus knew all along what the outcome was going to be!). The present form of these predictions, therefore, reflects the benefit of hindsight on the part of Mark or one of his predecessors. This is not to say, however, that Jesus had no inkling of what was in store; on the contrary, with the outworking of his ministry, together with the groundswell of opposition this generated, came a growing conviction that it would end in confrontation and death in one form or another (cf. the fate of John the Baptist). Further, Jesus may have hoped that God would vindicate him in some way if he remained faithful to the end (cf. 13:13; 15:34–36).

The designation 'Son of Man' remains a puzzle. Mark records Jesus using it in relation to his present ministry (2:10, 28), his forthcoming sufferings (8:31; 9:31; 10:33, 45) and his future vindication (8:38; 13:26; 14:62). And whilst it is questionable whether Jesus identified himself with the figure in the third of these categories, the first two clearly relate to him. But why does he use this enigmatic phrase? With respect to his ministry and sufferings, it may simply be a self-effacing way of referring to himself (cf. how we sometimes use 'one' instead of 'I') or, again, a form of self-designation in which Jesus sees himself as an example of humanity as a whole (cf. Psalm 8:4)—what he does, all are invited to do, and his fate is one that awaits others.

The sayings about the coming of the Son of Man in the future, however, do refer to a particular figure and clearly resonate with expectations current in the first century. The most fruitful source for both title and expectation is Daniel's vision in which one bearing the title 'Son of Man' appears from heaven and is instrumental in the fulfilment of God's saving purposes (Daniel 7:13). This vision and hope is developed further in the First Book of Enoch, where the Son of Man is equated with God's Messiah, although it remains unclear whether the relevant chapters ('the Similitudes') pre-date Jesus and were known to him. But if they weren't, he may well have been familiar with this 'endtime' or apocalyptic way of thinking in which God would intervene dramatically to bring the present corrupt order to a cataclysmic end, resulting in the vindication of the righteous and the punishment of the wicked (cf. Mark 13).

2 Ambassadors of Christ Read Mark 9:33–41

This rather disparate collection of traditions opens with another example of the disciples' inability to grasp the import of Jesus' words. Building on what he shared with them previously in 8:31—9:1, Jesus reiterates the conviction that his way, and, by implication, the way of discipleship, is the way of the cross. And yet we still find the disciples arguing over who is the greatest or most important of their number. We encounter a similar debate in the next chapter with James and John trying to secure positions of authority in Jesus' kingdom (10:35–45). And yet as incorrect and inappropriate an outlook as this is, it confirms they too believed something important was soon to take place, although, as we shall see, their hopes revolved around Jesus overthrowing the

Romans and re-establishing the kingdom of Israel.

Jesus responds to their desire for aggrandizement by calling them to follow his example (v. 35; cf. 10:43–45) and to reflect on the disposition of a child (vv. 36–37). Children are a teaching aid once more in 10:13–16, but in the present context it is unclear how they support Jesus' call for humility. Certainly, children were expected to be obedient and subservient to their seniors in Jesus' day, but verse 37 seems to be making an altogether different point (also v. 41). Either Jesus likens his followers to 'child-like ones' (cf. 10:15) who minister in humility or he encourages them to care for the weakest and most vulnerable members of society, namely, the young. Both alternatives are informed by the Jewish protocol of representation in which a man is present in the one authorized to stand in for him (i.e. his representative; e.g. child, envoy, messenger; cf. 12:1–12). Significantly, the verse closes with another insight into Jesus' self-understanding, namely, the conviction that he is God's ambassador.

News that there were itinerant exorcists using Jesus' name is perhaps not as surprising as we might first think (vv. 38–40). A similar practice is reflected in Acts 19:13–17 and, possibly, Acts 8:9–24, where Simon Magus is keen to tap into the miraculous power of Jesus' name. Further, we know that Jesus' followers believed themselves to have been commissioned by their master to participate in this aspect of his ministry and to continue it after his death (3:15; 6:7–13; 16:17). What is more striking is Jesus' response (vv. 39–40) in that he shuns the party-minded, myopic perspective of his disciple John and places these practices within the broader perspective of the kingdom.

3 The perils of insipid discipleship *Read Mark 9:42–49*

If the previous section concluded on a conciliatory note towards those outside Jesus' immediate group of disciples, the present collection of sayings presents uncompromising guidance for those counted amongst his followers. These verses present us with considerable textual difficulties and it is unclear at a number of points what constituted Mark's original text. This explains why verses 44 and 46 are missing from the NRSV, but included in the margin.

The unifying theme of the four sayings in verses 42–48 is guarding against whatever may cause disciples, or those influenced by them, to stumble on the journey of faith. In fact, the word translated here as 'to stumble' or 'stumbling block' became a technical term in Christian circles for apostasy or falling away. Verse 42 warns of the consequences of leading others astray, although the identity of 'these little ones who believe in me' remains unclear; the link with children in verses 36–37 is possible (as in Matthew 18:4–6), but a more general description of those young in the faith is more likely.

Whilst not wishing to diminish the force of the three sayings advocating mutilation of the body so that the life of the person can be saved, this is surely a case of Jesus using language hyperbolically. There is some evidence that the removal of a hand, foot or eye was practised as a form of punishment befitting the crime (cf. Deuteronomy 25:11–12; Exodus 21:24), but this remains conjecture. Jesus' point is surely that disciples must strive wholeheartedly to remain faithful to the gospel entrusted to them, for their actions have far-reaching consequences. However, we should note these verses do not imply that entry into God's kingdom is a reward, but only that life with God can be lost if disciples allow themselves to be distracted from following Jesus. The word translated 'hell' literally means 'Gehenna', a valley near Jerusalem which prior to the reforms of King Josiah was the site of child sacrifice to the god Moloch (2 Kings 23:10). In Jesus' time, it was the city's rubbish dump and, given its foulness of smell and inextinguishable flames, it provided a graphic symbol of what awaited the wicked and unfaithful. Note that it is the flames that are unquenchable, not the punishment!

Salt as a source of taste and an agent of preservation, purification and destruction provides the background for verses 49–50. The sense seems to be that disciples will be refined, as by fire (cf. 1 Corinthians 3:13–15), but with the hope that the salt of the gospel will purify, preserve and bring flavour to the life of faith.

4 The sanctity of marriage   *Read Mark 10:1–12*

In certain respects, the Pharisees' question to Jesus concerning divorce seems strange, for we know that the Jewish Law permitted the husband, but not his wife, this prerogative (cf. Deuteronomy 24:1–4). However, there was considerable debate in Jesus' time about what constituted grounds for divorce, whether it should be restricted to adultery or whether the husband should have greater freedom. Perhaps, then, this is the context for the current tradition.

Jesus' position is uncompromising, and after asking the Pharisees what Moses had to say on the subject, he explains that the provision allowing husbands to issue a bill of divorce was a concession for human obduracy and does not reflect God's will. In verses 6 to 9, he presents the scriptural basis for this contention (cf. Genesis 1:27; 2:24) and confirms that divorce is contrary to natural order and spiritual truth. Sexual union and the giving and being taken in marriage creates a bond that is God-given and should never be compromised. The NRSV's gender-inclusiveness may have shrouded Jesus' meaning in verse 9, where the word translated 'no one' literally means 'man' (singular) and refers to the husband. The sense is that husbands are enjoined not to take advantage of Moses' concession permitting them to divorce, but to honour the integrity and inviolability of the marital bond.

Human nature being what it is, there is good reason to think that the issue of whether divorce was permissible for followers of Jesus continued to be debated when Mark and the other evangelists were writing. This helps to explain the private instruction which the disciples receive afterwards (vv. 10–12; cf. 4:10; 9:28), where the implications of Jesus' teaching for husbands and wives, should they contemplate divorce, is clarified: both parties commit adultery against their 'former' spouse if they remarry. Given the Jewish Law did not permit wives to initiate divorce proceedings, this provision reflects the situation of the recipients of Mark's Gospel, who were under Roman jurisdiction. Further, it seems likely that when Jesus permits divorce in the case of unchastity (Matthew 19:9), the views of the Matthean community are being projected back onto Jesus to give them status and authority.

Finally, note that Jesus' uncompromising attitude towards marriage and divorce can be interpreted as an attempt to protect the position of women: where husbands are free to issue bills of divorce at whim, their wives have no security and little sense of personal worth.

5 Keys of the kingdom   *Read Mark 10:13–31*

The traditions about Jesus blessing the children (vv. 13–16) and encountering the wealthy man (vv. 17–31) are linked by a common concern with securing salvation. In characteristic fashion, the disciples are out of tune with Jesus and try to keep the children from him. It remains unclear why they were brought to Jesus in the first place and why his followers wished to keep them at a distance. Perhaps they were in need of healing (cf. 6:53–56). We are told that Jesus laid hands upon them and blessed them. This incident was used from early times to support infant baptism with 'do not stop them' (v. 14) becoming a baptismal formula (cf. Acts 8:36). But Jesus goes further and confirms the status of children by claiming that, of all people, it is they who model the right attitude towards God. We cannot be sure which childlike qualities he had in mind, but trust, imagination, enthusiasm and fascination are likely candidates.

We can identify at least three components in the next section which may originally have been independent of one another and brought together for thematic reasons at a later stage: the story of the rich man (vv. 17–22); Jesus' teaching about wealth (vv. 23–27); and his reassurance of the disciples (vv. 28–31). There is much in these verses worthy of note. First, it is interesting how Jesus reacts to being called 'good'; clearly, he believes that God alone merits this appellation and, whilst knowing himself to be called and commissioned by God, does not wish to be equated with him. Secondly, it is clear that observing laws, even the Ten Commandments (vv. 19–20; cf. Exodus 20:12–16), can leave one outside the kingdom unless matched by a willingness to abandon worldly securities and follow Jesus in a life of costly service. This insight would be particularly difficult for Jews who are encouraged in their scriptures to see wealth as a blessing from God (cf. Deuteronomy 28:1–14).

Thirdly, the saying about how difficult it is to enter the kingdom of God (v. 25) is clearly an exaggeration to make a point—and probably a humorous one at that! The issue is that salvation (v. 26), eternal life (vv. 17, 30) and the kingdom (vv. 23, 25), which presumably refer to the same reality, are gifts from God (v. 27) that cannot be earned, but only accepted and then responded to in a similarly gracious and God-inspired manner. And, finally, in a way that is entirely consistent with his ministry elsewhere, Jesus encourages his disciples to see this life, and in particular the relationships they enjoy, as the firstfruits of the harvest that will come to fruition in the fulness of God's time and purposes (vv. 28–30; cf. Romans 8:22–25; 2 Corinthians 1:22).

6 The way of the servant *Read Mark 10:35–45*

The request of James and John to be given positions of power alongside Jesus gives us a good clue to the kind of kingdom that his followers were hoping he would inaugurate (vv. 35–37). Clearly, it was one with socio-political implications, entailing the overthrow of the Roman authorities and the re-establishing of God's anointed one or Messiah as king and religious leader (cf. 11:1–11). This expectation has its roots in King David and in the belief that God would raise up from his stock another great leader who would bring deliverance and prosperity to his people (cf. 2 Samuel 7:8–16). Further, we know from the first-century work the Psalms of Solomon (chapters 17–18) that this hope was strong in Jesus' time—'See, Lord, and raise up for them their king, the son of David, to rule over your servant Israel in the time known to you, O God' (17:21). Hence the desire of the sons of Zebedee to be in positions of power and authority in the Messiah's newly formed government.

Jesus responds by refocusing their attention on the way of the cross and challenging them to share this with him. The metaphors of drinking from the cup of fate (Psalm 75:8; Jeremiah 49:12; Ezekiel 23:31–33) and of being baptized or overwhelmed by circumstances outside of one's control (Isaiah 21:4; 43:2) are drawn from the Hebrew scriptures and Jesus' meaning is clear: suffering and death await him and those who intend to share his faith and vocation. Interestingly, Jesus does not rule out future vindication by God (v. 40) and the reference here to his death as a 'baptism' (v. 38; cf. Luke 12:50) may have forged the link with Christian initiation (cf. Romans 6:3–4; Colossians 2:12).

Mark 10:45 is perhaps the most written-about verse of the whole Gospel. Jesus reinforces his conviction that only a life of service is a true measure of greatness (vv. 41–44) by offering the Son of Man (surely an indirect reference to himself) as a paradigm. Evidently, the notion of the Son of Man serving rather than being served was thought paradoxical, informed as it was by the elevated portrayal of this figure in Daniel and the Similitudes of Enoch (see notes on 9:30–32). Further, given that Jesus serves in God's name, his ministry discloses a serving God who ministers to his people's needs. Finally, verse 45b may well put us in touch with Jesus' understanding of his death: first, it would be the ultimate expression of his service (and, therefore, greatness); and, secondly, in some unexplained and perhaps inexplicable way, it would prove to be of saving benefit to others. Jesus not only foresees his ministry ending in death, but also appears to associate himself with the suffering servant figure of Isaiah 40–55 and the righteous martyrs of the faith found in 4 Maccabees 17 (a Greek-influenced Jewish work from the mid-first century AD)—a life offered or sacrificed for the sake of others (cf. 1 Corinthians 15:3).

GUIDELINES

We have reached another crisis point in our understanding of Jesus and the journey of discipleship. There can now be little doubt what following a vocation and ministering the gospel of God will mean for Jesus. In fact, the honesty with which he speaks of his imminent suffering and death is extraordinary. It betrays a level of awareness, a depth of self-knowledge and a capacity for faith that is as attractive as it is uncomfortable. For, if we're honest, few of us have the courage to live with the inevitability of death, even fewer of us to court it prematurely through taking unnecessary risks, and fewer still to believe that death can be redemptive (cf. 10:45).

Jesus' repeated reference to his death (e.g. 8:31; 9:30–32; 10:32–34), then, is remarkable and exposes the superficiality of our own faith as we confront matters of ultimate significance. Even the prospect of resurrection is a poor remedy when sacrificing the life we know for the possibility of one that may be no more than an edifice of hope. And yet it is precisely when Jesus is at his most human that his greatness is most transparent. Paradoxically, his vulnerability discloses a quality of being that transcends anything we have experienced and draws us into the mystery of a life formed by God.

Further, in the presence of such a life, we find ourselves embracing the dilemma of James and John (10:35–40)—for we too want a 'designer Messiah' who conforms to our expectations and will require of us only what we wish to give. Christology and discipleship are, indeed, intimately linked; and if Jesus is prepared to taste the cup of suffering and be overwhelmed by the baptism of death then so must we. But although Jesus has bared his soul and exposed our self-seeking motivations, still we must follow. Here, trust leads us forward and takes us beyond our understanding and desire for self-preservation. For we have entrusted too much of ourselves to Jesus to desert him now.

23–29 MARCH   MARK 10:46—12:17

1   The testimony of a 'seeing' blind man   Read Mark 10:46–52

The story of Bartimaeus is one of the great testimonies of faith recorded in the Gospels and Mark uses it to form a transition from his 'discipleship course' (see comment on 8:22–26) to the culmination of Jesus' ministry in Jerusalem. Here, as in 8:22–26, the contrast between different types of blindness and sight reinforces the conviction that only faith can discern who Jesus is within God's saving purposes.

Note how spatial imagery communicates the truth of what is unfolding. Initially, blind Bartimaeus is by the roadside (v. 46); but this is no ordinary road, for it is the route of Jesus' final journey and one which he predicted would embrace suffering, death and resurrection. This road, then, symbolizes for Mark the way of the cross, which is also the way of authentic discipleship. Bartimaeus hears of Jesus' approach, and his faith perceives God's anointed one who can deliver his people from oppression ('Jesus, Son of David, have mercy on me!'). It is probable that 'Son of David' would have been recognized as a title for God's Messiah in Jesus' time (cf. Psalms of Solomon 17:21).

Like others who discern God's hand upon Jesus (cf. 10:13–15), Bartimaeus' access is prevented by the spiritually blind; but Jesus will tolerate no gatekeepers as he invites Bartimaeus to approach him (v. 49). The 'seeing' blind man throws off his cloak, which as a beggar would constitute the sum of his worldly possessions; and, leaving all behind, he draws near (v. 50). Jesus' question ('What do you want me to do for you?') seems absurd for surely the answer is obvious—but faith only becomes truly liberating when exposed to the vulnerability of personal encounter and invested in the realization of concrete hopes. Bartimaeus' faith, then, leads him to Jesus in a way that physical sight never could— a paradox that is underlined when the eyes of the 'seeing' Bartimaeus are opened. And, finally, once Bartimaeus has experienced freedom from the dehumanizing effects of illness, destitution and despair, he chooses to become a disciple as he follows Jesus on the way.

No doubt the story of Bartimaeus has its roots in an historical incident, but Mark's skilful retelling of it creates a vehicle for divine encounter as faith enables us to draw near to Jesus and experience God's liberating presence—'Go; your faith has made you well' (v. 52).

2 Great expectations as Jesus enters Jerusalem   Read Mark 11:1–11

The so-called triumphal entry into Jerusalem stands in stark contrast to the secrecy of the previous chapters. The portrayal of Jesus as the long-awaited Son of David, riding in majesty, acclaimed by his subjects and in fulfilment of messianic prophecy (cf. Zechariah 9:9) as he claims his father's kingdom, appears to put an end to the rumours surrounding Jesus' identity that have circulated from the beginning. And yet even here all is not as it seems for there is much misunderstanding and pathos in these verses: hailed as God's anointed deliverer by those who would soon call for his execution, accursed of God (15:13–14; cf. Deuteronomy 21:22–23); a king of the Jews and yet without political or military aspirations; a dramatic entrance into God's holy city and temple which proves to be no more than a reconnaissance exercise.

The historical core of this tradition is difficult to recover. This is the first time Mark records Jesus going up to Jerusalem, although it is unlikely that the substance of chapters 11–15 all took place in the final week of Jesus' life; perhaps Mark has combined two or more visits to create a single episode (cf. John 2:13; 5:1; 12:12). Waving branches and shouting 'hosanna', as part of the recitation of the Hallel (Psalms 113–118; vv. 8–10), were characteristics of the autumn Feast of Tabernacles (harvest festival) and, possibly, the winter Feast of Hanukkah (rededication of the temple), rather than the Feast of Passover (deliverance from Egypt). And whilst Mark clearly understands 'hosanna' as a cry of praise and adulation, the Hebrew actually means something like 'save now' (cf. Psalm 118:25). Then, there is the matter of the colt (vv. 2–7). It was expected that pilgrims would travel on foot and, from what we can gather, this was Jesus' preferred means of travel; and yet he purposefully enters Jerusalem on an animal. Even a colt was considered a suitable ride for a king and it may well be that the requisitioning of the beast in the manner recorded is an example not so much of Jesus' supernatural knowledge as his royal prerogative.

What, then, are we to make of all this? First, Mark's presentation of this incident, with a partial lifting of the veil of ignorance, is consistent with his overarching plan in which the significance of Jesus for faith is reached through participation in the journey of discipleship, from beginning to end. From now on, we may share the faith of Bartimaeus (cf. 10:46–52) and acclaim Jesus as royal Messiah and Saviour; but what these categories mean and whether they are sufficient is yet to be seen. Secondly, if Jesus did enter Jerusalem as Mark narrates, riding in majesty, with the people preparing his way with their cloaks, and to shouts of 'Save now!' (*Hosanna*), then this would unquestionably have been interpreted as a messianic act with political implications. As prophesied and long-expected, God's anointed one has come to deliver his people from oppression and to re-establish the throne of David.

3 Faith, not sacrifice, gives access to God   *Read Mark 11:12–26*

These verses provide us with another example of Mark's 'sandwiching' technique. In this case, the cursing of the fig tree (vv. 12–14 and 20–25/6) encloses Jesus' action in the Jerusalem temple (vv. 15–19). Whatever gave rise to the former, Mark clearly interprets the cursing in a symbolic way reflecting God's judgment upon the worship of his people, which Jesus executes when in the temple.

Taken literally, the observation that Jesus' hunger could not be satisfied by a fig tree when out of season is no cause for surprise. His unprecedented action in cursing the tree, however, is extraordinary and invites a more spiritual or symbolic interpretation. From this perspective, it is significant that God's chosen people, Israel, are referred to in the Hebrew scriptures as barren fig trees when they are unfaithful to God and bring judgment upon themselves (Jeremiah 8:13; Hosea 9:10; Micah 7:1). It seems likely, therefore, that Mark is drawing upon this background here in presenting the cursing as a form of prophetic act symbolizing God's judgment.

But what exactly has brought about God's judgment? There are a number of possibilities, including the corruption of the temple priesthood, the commercialization of the temple and the hypocrisy of exterior religiosity without a corresponding moral commitment. One would expect Jesus' action in the temple to point us in the right direction, but this is difficult to assess, for the money changers and sellers of livestock were all part of the sacrificial system as defined in the Jewish Law. By venting his righteous indignation against those who service the 'system' and by quoting a passage from Isaiah which affirms the universal compass of God's grace and favour ('for all people', v. 17; cf. Isaiah 56:7), it seems probable that Jesus' concern was principally about access to God. The sacrificial system, restricted to one place in Jerusalem, controlled by a religious élite and open to commercial exploitation, was an inappropriate vehicle for establishing and maintaining relationship with God.

Certainly, this is how Mark interprets the happening, for faith in God (vv. 22–24), hope-filled expectant prayer (v. 25) and a life reflecting God's forgiveness (v. 26) are the channels for divine encounter and for realizing God's sovereign presence. Interestingly, Jesus announces that faith will precipitate the levelling of the spiritual landscape and a corresponding opening up of access to God with the destruction of 'this mountain' (v. 23) into the depths of the sea. 'This mountain' can only mean the Temple Mount, the gateway to God; and its demolition would have the effect of the earth becoming 'full of the knowledge of the Lord as the waters cover the sea' (Isaiah 11:9).

4 Who is able to speak for God? *Read Mark 11:27–33*

The setting for this controversy between Jesus and representatives from the chief priests, the scribes and the elders is the temple. These groups constituted the principal religious authorities in Jerusalem at that time and comprised the supreme Jewish court known as the Sanhedrin. Not surprisingly, the manner of Jesus' arrival in Jerusalem (11:1–11) and his subsequent conduct (11:15–18) had precipitated a crisis over authority and, in particular, over who is able to speak for God. Further, it is conceivable that Jesus' entire ministry is under scrutiny at this juncture as he is challenged to defend his self-assumed position as a religious leader with a reputation for teaching, healing and associating with those on the margins of society.

The practice of responding to a question (v. 28) with a counter-question (vv. 29–30) is characteristic of Jewish debating technique. Jesus' allusion to John the Baptist here may simply be a skilful sidestep to shift attention from himself; however, a more likely explanation is that he wished to come under the auspices of John's reputation as a man of God. The implication is that if John was authorized by God, so was he.

The shrewdness and dexterity of Jesus' answer is spelt out in verses 31–32, where his opponents find themselves facing a dilemma revolving around two major issues. First, the standing and relative importance of, on the one hand, charismatic and, on the other, institutional authority. John and Jesus stood outside the established religious authorities of the day. As far as we know, they hadn't been formally trained and, consequently, hadn't been authorized to speak on behalf of any group; however, they claimed divine authority as those commissioned directly by God, rather than indirectly by religious bodies claiming divine legitimization.

This was as extremely difficult an area then as it is today, with the excesses of unfettered religious enthusiasm and the capacity of structures for corruption and for stifling the divine Spirit etched onto every chapter of religious history. But controls exist and this was the second problem. For unless those in authority possess the power of enforcement, their ability to influence is dependent on the permission and cooperation of others. And given the Roman occupation, Jesus' opponents could not afford to ignore popular opinion which recognized the charismatic authority of John (as a prophet; v. 32). Faced with the alternative of either endorsing John's ministry, thereby undermining their own power base and opening themselves to the accusation of failing to heed the Baptist's call for repentance, or risking disapproval and worse at the hands of a volatile and greatly enlarged pilgrim population in Jerusalem, they attempt to sit on the fence. Their silence may reflect a genuine uncertainty over John and Jesus, or it may communicate most eloquent rejection; for Mark, it is the latter.

5 A window into Jesus' self-understanding? *Read Mark 12:1–12*

This parable affords us one of our closest insights into how Jesus viewed his relationship to God, his ministry and his fate. We need to remember that interpretations of Jesus emerging after his death are likely to have influenced the evangelists' presentations, making it difficult to distinguish between Jesus' self-understanding and later assessments of him. And whilst there are signs of such reinterpretation in this parable, notably with the inclusion of Psalm 118:22–23 (vv. 10–11) to explain Jesus' rejection by fellow Jews and, presumably, to vindicate his followers (cf. Acts 4:11; Ephesians 2:20; 1 Peter 2:7), the remainder has a ring of authenticity about it. The parable of the wicked tenants, of all the parables, invites allegorical interpretation. We know that the vineyard was a recognized symbol for Israel and in Isaiah 5:1–7 we find a similar allegory, with the prophet condemning God's people by likening their disobedience to the fruitlessness of a vineyard. Jesus' parable also suggests a controversial setting, possibly over authority (cf. 11:27–33) and the continued failure of the religious hierarchy to be open to the Spirit of God (cf. Luke 19:41–44).

What, then, does this parable tell us about Jesus' self-understanding? First, it suggests that Jesus associated himself with those Spirit-inspired messengers (i.e. the owner's slaves) who were rejected by the leaders of God's people, Israel (i.e. the vineyard tenants; cf. 6:4). Significantly, however, Jesus does not characterize himself as a 'slave', but, constituting the final initiative, as the owner's only son and heir (vv. 6–7). Here, it is not so much the intimacy of sonship as the authority it bestows upon Jesus that is in view. It appears that Jesus believed himself to occupy a unique and final role within God's initiatives to save his people.

Further, the parable suggests that Jesus recognized his ministry would end in rejection and death. No doubt the fate of John the Baptist will have forced him to confront this possibility, and stories of the martyrdoms of the great Hebrew prophets (e.g. Isaiah, Jeremiah and Ezekiel) were current and plentiful. In addition, Jesus may well have known of Honi, a Galilean charismatic miracle worker, who was stoned in Jerusalem a few decades earlier. What is equally significant, however, is that verse 8 suggests a death within the walls of the vineyard; yet Jesus was executed outside of the walls of Jerusalem! It is difficult to think this detail would have been introduced if the parable was a product of the early Church.

6 Jesus and the two kingdoms   *Read Mark 12:13–17*

These verses contain the first in a group of four questions (also vv. 19–23, v. 28 and v. 35) that Mark presents together. Their purpose was to trap Jesus into error and so to undermine his authority and influence. Significantly, however, the quality of his answers shifts attention away from the suspect motivations of his inquisitors onto Jesus as a man of wisdom and a teacher of truth. The first trap set for him concerns the payment of a poll tax that was imposed on the inhabitants of Judea, Samaria and Idumea when formed into a Roman province in AD6. As we can imagine, Jews viewed this tax as an imposition and objected to the erosion of their national identity by being parcelled together with alien peoples. Further, the Roman denarius, the legal tender for the payment of the tax, bore the image of the emperor. And, according to Jewish Law, the engraving of any human likeness was forbidden, and the casting of one's image on a coin was regarded as idolatrous.

Jesus finds himself on the horns of a dilemma: to advocate payment would cost him popular support amongst his fellow Jews; to renounce it would cast him in the mould of a political agitator and probably lead to his arrest by the Romans. However, the profundity of Jesus' answer transcends such constraints and communicates a timeless truth concerning the relationship between faith and life.

And yet we must acknowledge that Jesus' meaning here remains a matter of debate. Some have seen in these words Jesus' advocacy of a 'two kingdoms' theology where the demands of, on the one hand, the kingdom of God and, on the other, the kingdoms of this world are neither mutually incompatible nor impinge one upon the other. Even a superficial knowledge of Jesus' message and ministry, however, highlights the implausibility of this proposal, for his vision was rooted in helping others to discover God's justice, truth and mercy in this life and not just in the next. On the contrary, Jesus' response clearly acknowledges the rightful demands of God and state; but there can be little doubt where his allegiances reside should there be a conflict of loyalties. The image of the emperor may have been stamped on each denarius, but the image of God is etched on every human soul.

GUIDELINES

The readings of the past week witness the beginning of Jesus' passion. For passion is about losing control, becoming vulnerable and being at the mercy of others. And although never free of expectations and other constraints, Jesus was largely able to pursue his ministry unimpeded when in Galilee. With his approach to Jerusalem, however, all this changed. Blind Bartimaeus signals the transition when he petitions Jesus in explicitly messianic terms, 'Son of David' (10:47–48). Now Jesus is typecast, as the hopes of the pilgrim people of God, and especially their longing that God would raise up a saviour to perform a new exodus by breaking the grip of Roman rule, are projected onto him. How much Jesus encouraged such speculation is now difficult to determine; but one thing is clear: control of his destiny soon passed out of his hands. Then, as now, people made of him what they wanted and the pathos of Jesus' predicament emerges with the Jewish and Roman authorities arresting and executing him on the basis of messianic pretensions that others entertained on his behalf. This is the anatomy of powerlessness as Jesus' life is placed on the sacrificial altar of public opinion and political expediency.

Jesus, then, finds himself facing opposition on all fronts and needing to defend his vision of God's kingdom against those feeling increasingly threatened by his unwillingness to conform to their stereotypes and by the authority he continued to possess after the bastions of power disowned him. And as we search for the flame that fires Jesus' ministry, one phrase comes to mind, 'Have faith in God' (11:22). Perhaps it is here that opposites meet, as we encounter God in humanity and humanity in God. What kind of faith is this? It is a naked trust in God's covenantal faithfulness and an overwhelming conviction that God is for us and can be found in relationships and patterns of life reflecting his ways. This is a faith unfettered by doctrinal controls and informed by the limitless grace of God—it is a 'mountain-moving' faith (11:23) that participates in the omnipotence of God. Little wonder that Jesus was celebrated as the pioneer and perfecter of faith (Hebrews 12:2; contrary to the NRSV, there is no 'our' in the original Greek!).

As we reflect on this dimension of Jesus' life, we soon recognize here something that we need desperately. For without sharing the faith of Jesus it is impossible to find the radical freedom to live in the midst of the manifold pressures exerted by political, economic, social and religious authorities, seeking to conform and manipulate, and still take responsibility for own decisions and destinies. Without this faith we are unable to follow Jesus in the way of the cross—of passion and costly love.

1   The God of the living   *Read Mark 12:18–27*

From what we can gather, the belief that God would bodily resurrect his people from Sheol, the shadowy existence that awaits all at death, came to expression within the Jewish faith at a relatively late stage. We can see signs of it taking shape in the Psalms with believers struggling to make sense of suffering and death in the light of God's love for and unconditional commitment to them (e.g. Psalms 30 and 88). Further, with the increasing influence of Greek culture and ideas upon the Jewish way, belief in the immortality of the soul was absorbed into speculation about the afterlife during the intertestamental period (in works such as Wisdom and 4 Maccabees). However, it was the need for justice and vindication for those Jews who had been persecuted and killed as they refused to compromise their faith that finally gave birth to the conviction that God would raise them up to eternal life and punish their enemies (Isaiah 26:19; Daniel 12:1–3; Psalms of Solomon 13–15; 2 Maccabees 7).

But as this passage from Mark makes clear, not all Jews subscribed to this belief. The evangelist confirms what the Jewish historian Josephus also reports, namely, that, unlike their Pharisaic counterparts, the Sadducees did not believe in the resurrection. Constituting the religious aristocracy of the day, their conservative outlook made them suspicious of new developments; and even under Roman rule, they enjoyed a standard of living which gave them little cause to despair of this life!

Their question to Jesus concerning the resurrection (vv. 19–23) assumes the principle of levirate marriage specified in Deuteronomy 25:5–10, whereby a Jewish man is guaranteed an heir by requiring his brothers to marry his wife should he die without a son. Although the Sadducees cite Moses as their authority (i.e. the five books of Moses, including Deuteronomy), Jesus criticizes them for knowing neither the scriptures nor the God to whom they bear witness (v. 24). We should note that Jesus' answer is primarily a rebuttal of what he considered to be a largely irrelevant issue and cannot be interpreted as his definitive statement on post-mortem existence. However, in addition to reflecting the current view about sharing an angelic existence, it suggests that the resurrected life will neither be regulated by the Mosaic Law nor

general one about the dangers of external religiosity masking sinister conduct and morally bankrupt motivations (cf. 11:12–26). Their practice of exploiting widows is clearly deplorable and may refer to unscrupulous estate management by the religious authorities.

A widow is also the subject of the final tradition in this section (vv. 41–44), which continues the theme of the previous one, namely, that appearances can be deceptive and need not reveal a person's true self. In this case, the issue is giving to God or, at least, to the religious structure claiming divine authority (i.e. the temple). As usual, Jesus' insight is both penetrating and disturbing: generosity is not a measure of the contribution, but a condition of the heart.

4 End-time predictions (part 1) *Read Mark 13:1–13*

Chapter 13 is a remarkable piece of writing, timetabling the final countdown before God intervenes decisively through his heavenly Messiah, the Son of Man, to save the faithful from a corrupt humanity's collision course with disaster. We find examples of this kind of apocalyptic speculation in the Hebrew scriptures (e.g. Daniel) and it was widespread in the first century. Many influences can be identified within this genre, including concern over God's non-activity in the world and his failure to fulfil covenantal promises, a desire to imbue the present with meaning, and a longing to know the mind of God not only in the past and present but also in the future.

Apocalyptic writing invites hearers to discover their own situation within its imagery and allusions, and so to redeem life by locating it within sacred time—the outworkings of salvation history. Of the various end-time overtures rehearsed in chapter 13, references to the destruction of the temple (v. 2) and its desecration (v. 14) are identifiable events, although it is unclear whether Mark writes before or after their fulfilment (the temple was destroyed by fire in AD70). This issue is one of the determining factors for dating the Gospel.

Did Jesus compose this apocalyptic monologue either in its entirety or in part? There is little reason to doubt that some of the material originates with him, including quite possibly the prediction of the temple's destruction (a view shared by other Jews), the warning over imminent persecution and apostasy, together with the belief that God would intervene through his heavenly agent. However, not only is the extended discourse style uncharacteristic of Jesus (if the first three Gospels are any guide), but also the worldview underpinning it goes against the grain of Jesus' largely positive and life-affirming attitude towards this world as a place for divine encounter and experiencing God's blessings. In the light of this, the current form of the discourse suggests editorial reworking and may contain considerable supplementary material of either Jewish or Christian provenance.

Mark may already have alluded to Jesus' conviction concerning the destruction of the temple in 11:23, where 'this mountain' refers to the Temple Mount. The significance of this event is usually understood in terms of judgment upon Israel or, at least, upon its corrupt religious hierarchy; however, the import for Jesus may have been more one of demonstrating the redundancy of the temple sacrificial system for mediating access to God. And yet before the decisive events of the end-time take place, disciples must prepare themselves for the 'birth pangs', including religious charlatans masquerading as Jesus (v. 6), political unrest (v. 7), and natural disasters (v. 8). Evidently, Jesus did not foresee the cataclysmic consummation of all things in his own lifetime; and, after 2,000 years of Christian history, which generation has been free of such incidents?

5 End-time predictions (part 2) *Read Mark 13:14–37*

One of the striking characteristics of apocalyptic timetables is the way in which future events are thought to be predetermined. The die has been cast, either by God from the beginnings of time or by the effects of sinful generations now beyond redemption. According to Jesus, the placement of the 'desolating sacrilege' (v. 14)—a phrase taken from Daniel 12:11 where it refers to the altar to Zeus constructed in the Jerusalem temple by Antiochus Epiphanes in 168BC—is an example of this phenomenon. Whether Jesus had the temple's destruction in mind or some other act of desecration is unclear.

God's intervention is prompted by the need to save the elect or a surviving remnant (v. 20). Evidently, without divine assistance no one, not even the upright and faithful, would be left alive. One way in which apocalyptic writing highlights both the disordering effects of human sinfulness and the corresponding displeasure of God is by depicting the disruption of the natural order (vv. 24–25; cf. Isaiah 13:10; 34:4; Ezekiel 32:7–8; Joel 2:10; 3:15; Amos 8:9). These happenings provide the backdrop for the coming of the heavenly Son of Man (vv. 26–27). The book of Daniel (7:13–14) once again supplies the imagery for God's deliverer, a cosmic messiah empowered to implement the divine will, with or without human cooperation. The gathering together of the remnant of faithful Israel also expresses a hope found in the Hebrew scriptures (cf. Isaiah 11:11; 43:5–6).

Do these verses reflect Jesus' understanding? One school of thought is that Jesus did expect God to intervene in human history and believed his death would act as a trigger for this intervention. Certainly, his mode of entry into Jerusalem, coupled with his conduct in the temple at a time when Jewish nationalistic and messianic fervour would have been high, suggests a desire to orchestrate a confrontation and so to precipitate a crisis. As we shall see, Jesus succeeded on this count.

The parables contained in verses 28–31 and 32–37 pick up the flavour of Jesus' apocalyptic discourse even if they weren't originally a part of it. The pattern of nature as exemplified by a fig tree demonstrates the inevitability of God's judgment and consummation of all things, whilst the parable of the house owner reinforces one of the principle functions of apocalyptic writing, namely, to encourage faithfulness, obedience and conscientiousness.

6 The ambiguity of intimacy   *Read Mark 14:1–11*

From this point the order of events narrated by Mark possesses a coherence that reflects both regular retelling and a correspondence with what actually happened. In these verses, we find the plot to kill Jesus (vv. 1–2, 10–11) enveloping his anointing at Bethany (vv. 3–9). Mark has already informed us of the religious leaders' intention to silence Jesus (e.g. 3:6; 11:18; 12:12), presumably because he undermined their own authority, threatened to destabilize the fragile peace and, perhaps, was genuinely thought to be a false prophet.

Judas' willingness to hand Jesus over may well have persuaded his opponents to throw caution to the wind (cf. v. 2) and to act during the festival of Passover and Unleavened Bread (originally two separate feasts, but amalgamated later; cf. 2 Chronicles 35:17). Christian tradition has cast Judas in the mould of the malevolent, avaricious disciple who betrays his Lord with a kiss. Yet the word translated 'betray' (v. 10) need carry no pejorative overtones and may simply mean 'hand over'. His motivations for leading the religious authorities to Jesus when in a secluded place are now out of reach. But this seems to be the extent of the crime; the rest is interpretation. And in the light of this, one wonders whether Judas has been made into something of a scapegoat, bearing the guilt of all those who betray Jesus, as he is cast out from the community of faith and destroyed as a form of recompense or atonement (cf. Matthew 27:3–10).

The anointing of Jesus is one of the most powerful and enigmatic stories recorded in the Gospels. The woman's actions can readily be accommodated within the social protocols of the day; however, the opulence of her gesture in using costly ointments was extraordinary and for this reason received a mixed response. For some, no doubt indignant at such waste, it was excessive, financially irresponsible and contrary to Jesus' priorities and commitments. And yet in spite of this, Jesus defends her. We can only assume that, whereas onlookers reacted to what she did, Jesus discerned her motivations and judged them to be worthy. Perhaps, as with the woman in Luke 7:36–50, he recognized an expression of love and devotion that was truly inspirational and exemplary. Certainly, this anonymous follower is promised the highest acclaim (v. 9).

However, there may be more to this story than first appears. For one thing, the anointing anticipates Jesus' death and becomes the preparation of his corpse that the empty tomb prevents (cf. 16:1). For another, anointing with oil was a means of investing power or communicating status and blessing. Israelite kings were anointed (e.g. 1 Kings 1:39; Psalm 89:20) and God's future saviour would be similarly endowed ('Messiah' literally means 'anointed'). Whether these associations were in the minds of Jesus and the woman we shall never know, but they clearly resonate with Mark's convictions. For the woman's faith not only perceives the way of Jesus to be the way of the cross, but also confirms that Jesus' true identity only becomes manifest through his Passion.

GUIDELINES

Finding God at the extremes of human experience is the theme running through this week's readings. A faith that trusts God not only for this life, but also for the next; a commitment to love both the God whom we cannot see and our neighbours whose presence is only too obvious; the challenge to stick with Jesus when he courts controversy, disturbs the status quo of religious complacency, and requires his followers to embrace the crisis associated with the realization of God's sovereign reign on earth.

Living in the present when it is invested with so much significance and full of so many demands has the effect of polarizing human response: some are drawn into the vision of an eternal now, of the dawning of salvation, whilst others are incapable or unwilling to embrace this invitation to authentic life. And as we have seen, Jesus precipitates such polarization because his life communicates a quality of human being and an investment in God that is at the same time inspirational and threatening. In one sense, his faith is too strong for he refuses to compromise or seek a less confrontational approach. Faith must be tested in the crucible of human experience and so, by implication, must the God who is believed in.

That such intensity of faith and human being should meet with outright opposition is only to be expected—for it is easier to destroy what threatens us than to allow it to destroy or transform us. But what is remarkable is the radical freedom that some found in Jesus' presence. And here the irresponsible generosity of the anonymous woman who anoints Jesus is pre-eminent. For this gesture speaks of one who is truly being herself and expressing a quality of love that is constrained neither by the desire for self-preservation nor concern for popular opinion. And in case we are tempted to think this demonstration of devotion rather self-indulgent and inappropriate, it is worth remembering that in the Gospel story it precedes and prepares Jesus for an even more extravagant and public manifestation.

Few of us find it easy to be true to our authentic selves and to live wholeheartedly and unreservedly in the present. But this is the inheritance of faith that Jesus bequeaths to those who choose to follow him in the way of the cross.

6–12 APRIL   **MARK 14:12—16:8**

1 Jesus entrusts his ministry to the disciples
Read Mark 14:12–31

The foreknowledge attributed to Jesus in these verses is extraordinary, including predictions of betrayal and denial by his followers (vv. 18–21; 27–31). Had things been as Mark records here it is difficult to understand why Jesus didn't withdraw from Jerusalem and avoid arrest. Unless, of course, he intended this course of events to come about, in which case Judas should be recast in a different light in that his 'handing over' becomes essential to the story of salvation. A more likely explanation is that these predictions reflect a later stratum of interpretation which attempts to give a sense of divine coherence to the course of Jesus' final days. In this way, the impression is given that whatever happened was all part of a preordained divine plan.

The institution of the Lord's Supper is one of the most difficult events in Jesus' life for us to appreciate now. It has precipitated such a rich feast of theological meaning and liturgical expression that it is extremely hard to distinguish between Jesus' intention and later interpretation. We know that meals and table fellowship were an integral component of Jesus' ministry. They were a celebration of God's sustenance and saving presence (e.g. 2:18–20; 6:31–44; 8:1–10; Luke 7:31–35), a tangible demonstration of God's acceptance and reconciliation of those on the margins (e.g. 2:15–17), and a foretaste of the abundant blessings that communion with God would yield in the future (14:25; cf. Isaiah 25:6–10).

Although Mark presents Jesus' final meal as a Passover commemoration (v. 12–13; in contrast to John 13:1), this may reflect a later attempt to interpret Jesus' death in the light of the Passover sacrifice. Certainly, the Passover meal, with the symbolic use of foods to remember and re-enact God's great act of salvation when the Israelites 'passed over' from slavery into freedom, provides a rich interpretative matrix for the last supper (cf. Exodus 12:1–14; Deuteronomy 16:1–3). However, it is questionable whether Jesus wished his followers to understand his death as a new Passover.

For one thing, the word 'is', which identifies bread with Jesus' body and wine with his blood (vv. 22–24), has no equivalent in Aramaic; and, in any case, a Jew would find the prospect of drinking blood abhorrent (Leviticus 17:10–16; Deuteronomy 12:15–28). Jesus intends the bread and wine to *represent* something and not to *become* what is represented. Again, the word translated 'body' (v. 22) does not relate to a part of Jesus, but constitutes the entire person and may be used here to encapsulate his life and ministry. Further, comparison with 1 Corinthians 11:25, the earliest witness to Jesus' words of institution, suggests that the principal association is between wine and covenant, and only by implication between wine and blood.

Unfortunately, space does not permit a full discussion of these important issues, but we may well be closer to Jesus' meaning when we understand the words and actions associated with the bread as a commissioning of the disciples and an entrusting to them of his God-given vocation. The words and actions associated with the wine celebrate the new relationship between God and humanity realized through Jesus' ministry and death, and finding fulfilment in God's future (v. 25).

2 Gethsemane and the humanity of Jesus *Read Mark 14:32–52*

Although it is difficult to understand how Jesus' anguish in the garden of Gethsemane was recorded, the story is surprisingly well attested (Matthew 26:36–46; Luke 22:39–46; Hebrews 5:7–8; cf. John 12:27; 14:31; 18:11). It provides us with some of the most intimate insights into Jesus' relationship with God and how he viewed his vocation. We have already hinted that the portrayal of Jesus as one who predicts the course of his Passion (e.g. 8:31–32; 9:30–31; 10:32–34), together with the desertion of his followers (e.g. 14:17–21, 26–31), is a construct of the evangelist, designed to give a sense of divine foreknowledge and purpose to otherwise chaotic and potentially faith-destroying events. And whilst there is evidence of this editorial reworking in the Gethsemane tradition (e.g. vv. 41–42), we encounter a dramatically different Jesus within these verses.

Indeed, the Jesus of Gethsemane exhibits a depth of humanity that is more demanding and profound than his most public demonstrations of power. He confronts death not as a temporary glitch on the way to resurrection glory ('... and after three days rise again', 8:31; 9:31; 10:34), but as a stark reality that threatens to destroy everything. His sense of vocation is tested to the limits as he is overwhelmed by anxiety and grief at the prospect of facing the hour of testing and consuming the cup of fate (cf. 10:38–39). 'Abba', the Aramaic for 'my father' or 'our father', communicates familial intimacy and, presumably, is recorded here in the original language to emphasize that it was characteristic of Jesus' way of addressing God (also Matthew 6:9; cf. Romans 8:15; Galatians 4:6).

Jesus' petition, 'Abba, Father, for you all things are possible; remove this cup from me; yet, not what I want, but what you want' (v. 36), concentrates into one sentence what must have been a gradual movement towards acceptance and resolution. The quality of Jesus' faith exhibited here is extraordinary: a childlike trust in the divine omnipotence of God (cf. 9:23; 10:27; 11:22–24) and a radical obedience enabling him to entrust his future to God and to abandon life itself in pursuit of a vocation (cf. 8:34–37; 13:13). Significantly, it is Christ's obedience that Paul stresses when discussing the saving effects of the cross (Romans 5:17–19; Philippians 2:8). The account of Jesus' betrayal and arrest also possesses a ring of authenticity (vv. 43–52), although it contains more questionable components (e.g. vv. 51–52). The armed mob acts, at least informally, under the auspices of the Sanhedrin. Surprisingly, given Jesus' activities in the temple, he is not readily identifiable by his captors and has to be pointed out. Although Judas' mode of betrayal seems unnecessarily heartless, a kiss was a recognized way for a pupil to greet a rabbi. As we shall see, the disciples' desertion of Jesus may not have been as final as these verses suggest; here, in accordance with Mark's presentation throughout, their response is predetermined (vv. 49–50; cf. 14:26–31). Interestingly, we find a more positive assessment of Peter, James and John on the lips of Jesus in verse 38, where their willingness to stand by him is recognized.

3 Jesus is tried and sentenced   Read Mark 14:53–65; 15:1–15

This long section, narrating Jesus' encounters with Jewish and Roman authorities, together with Peter's denial, is full of problems. Mark's record of his trial before the Sanhedrin repeatedly contravenes the rules stipulated in the *Mishnah* (an authoritative supplement to the Jewish Law), which although not compiled until AD 200 draws on older traditions: trials must be held in a special hall on the Temple Mount and could not be conducted during feasts or at night; defendants were innocent until proven guilty and only needed to answer accusations which could be substantiated; convictions required at least two corroborative testimonies; a verdict could not be reached before a second meeting of the Sanhedrin on a separate day. And then what was the charge meriting the death penalty? Does it concern Jesus' pronouncements about the destruction and rebuilding of the temple (v. 58) or his messianic pretensions (vv. 61–62)? If it is the former, why doesn't Mark record Jesus making this claim (13:1–2 is a prediction not an undertaking; cf. John 2:19)? If it is the latter, claiming to be the Messiah was neither a capital offence nor blasphemous (the Messiah was not God, but God's human agent). The evangelist's account of Jesus' meeting with Pilate is hardly more convincing (15:1–15). It portrays the Roman prefect as an indecisive, ponderous and conciliatory man when, according to the Jewish historian Josephus, he was 'inflexible, merciless and obstinate'. Further, there is no evidence of the custom of releasing prisoners at festivals, and the likelihood of Pilate liberating a committed murderer and political agitator is extremely small.

What, then, are we to make of all this? There is good reason to think that Mark has heavily reworked his traditions to serve both his theological interests and apologetic concerns. We notice how as Jesus' death draws closer, so the veil over his identity is withdrawn (vv. 61–62). Equally, the evangelist emphasizes the culpability of the Jews, who had become antagonistic towards Christianity (cf. Matthew 27:19–26; Luke 23:4–16; John 18:28–38; 19:4–16), whilst reducing the involvement of the Roman authorities, who continued in power and posed a real threat to the future of the Christian faith.

And, although we cannot now construct what happened to Jesus in any detail, it does seem likely that he was arrested by the Jewish authorities and faced the Sanhedrin informally to establish the nature of his ministry and to assess his threat with respect to their religious authority. We cannot rule out here a genuine motivation to give Jesus a hearing, but we must also recognize their desire to do away with him. The grounds for this remain unclear, although the belief that Jesus undermined their authority and threatened the fragile peace are likely contenders. We can only assume that the Sanhedrin would have executed Jesus had it possessed the powers to do so. However, that Jesus was handed over to the Roman authorities suggests this wasn't the case. Pilate's decision to accede to the Sanhedrin's request would have been motivated by political considerations. Clearly, if Jesus had committed treason by claiming to be 'the King of the Jews' (vv. 2, 9, 12), this would have posed a very real threat to Roman rule and would need to be dealt with in the customary manner to avoid unrest and possible insurrection. This would have been even more necessary given the strong nationalistic fervour and vastly swollen population of Jerusalem associated with the Passover festival.

4 Peter's denial; Jesus crucified   *Read Mark 14:66–72; 15:16–32*

There is good reason to believe the incident concerning Peter's denial of Jesus is rooted in historical fact. It is highly unlikely that the early Church would have created such a story, especially as Peter was one of the principal leaders and the denial portrays him in decidedly unflattering terms. On a positive note, it suggests the disciples' abandonment of Jesus was not as complete as Mark indicates (cf. 14:50). Surely Peter wouldn't have risked shadowing him into the courtyard of the high priest's residence if this had been the case. Whether the detail concerning the cock is original and why Peter's Galilean accent should have given him away when Jerusalem was full of pilgrims is impossible to say.

There is no question that crucifixion was a gruesome form of execution, reserved by the Romans for perpetrators of particularly serious crimes. Victims were made to carry their own crossbar, stripped and fixed to the wooden structure either by nails or ropes. The legs were usually bent to make it harder to breathe and the arms were fixed at the wrist (and not through the palms as many religious artists would have us believe). Death was often an extremely prolonged affair and usually resulted from asphyxiation, sometimes after many days. On top of all this, there was the public humiliation and disgrace, together with whatever the executioners and onlookers meted out.

Details of Jesus' crucifixion may well provide further evidence of the disciples' continuing commitment to him—who else would have recorded them? It appears that the charge brought against him of claiming to be 'the King of the Jews' (v. 26) was the source of additional suffering, both before (vv. 17–20) and during (vv. 29–32) his ordeal on the cross. We know next to nothing about Simon of Cyrene (v. 21), and his being pressed into carrying Jesus' cross was highly unusual. Perhaps Jesus was so weakened by his floggings and abuse at the hands of the Roman soldiers that he was in danger of dying before sentence could be carried out. The whereabouts of Golgotha (v. 22) is now not known, although the name, meaning 'the skull', suggests a hill on the outskirts of Jerusalem. The provision of wine mixed with myrrh to ease the pain must have come from one of Jesus' followers (v. 23). And it appears the mockery of the Roman soldiers was augmented by that of passers-by, members of the Sanhedrin and even those crucified with him (vv. 29–32).

And yet in spite of all this pain and anguish, it is difficult not to interpret Mark's presentation of Jesus' crucifixion as a sort of victory. For the evangelist, there is genuine pathos here: the one who is taunted to come down from the cross to save his life and convince his audience of his royal and messianic credentials is indeed the Saviour of God's people, as the one who prophesied the destruction of the temple becomes the source of atonement and the new place of divine encounter.

5   The death and burial of Jesus   *Read Mark 15:33–47*

Although Mark's theological interests can be discerned in his retelling of Jesus' death and burial, there is good reason to believe that his account is largely factual. In contrast to Luke (23:34, 43, 46) and John (19:26–28, 30), Jesus makes only one utterance from the cross (v. 34) and this echoes the opening verse of Psalm 22. It is impossible to say whether this heart-rending cry of desolation signals the end of Jesus' faith or is yet another profound demonstration of it (as he remains convinced that there is a God worth appealing to!). The confusion over Elijah (vv. 35–36) could only occur in Hebrew and not in Aramaic as

Mark records (cf. Matthew 27:46), whilst the belief that the prophet could be invoked in times of trouble is attested in later Jewish sources and is presumably a ramification of his translation into heaven (2 Kings 2:11–12). The offer of wine (v. 36) may well be historical, even though this detail can be found in what would become one of the great Passion Psalms of the Church (Psalm 69:21).

Strictly speaking, the Sabbath had already begun when Joseph of Arimathea petitions Pilate for Jesus' body (vv. 42–45). The Jewish Law required the burial of malefactors on the day of death (Deuteronomy 21:22–23) and, although the Romans sometimes left their victims to decompose on the cross, it was not unheard of for them to respect Jewish sensibilities and release the corpse; hence Joseph's courageous initiative. Mark tells us that Joseph was a 'respected member of the council' and one who was 'waiting expectantly for the kingdom of God' (v. 43). Matthew adds that he was a disciple of Jesus (27:57), a secret one according to John (19:38), who Luke stresses did not agree with the council's decision to kill Jesus. It sounds as if Joseph was a member of the Sanhedrin who, if not a follower of Jesus, identified with him to the extent that he was willing to hand over his unused family tomb and risk rebuttal by Pilate and ostracism by his Jewish counterparts.

Two features of Jesus' death are central for Mark's presentation. The first concerns the tearing of the curtain (v. 38), which must refer to the one hanging at the entrance to the Holy of Holies, the locus of God's presence on earth (Exodus 26:31–35). Only the high priest was permitted to enter this place and then only once a year to make atonement for sins (Leviticus 16:29–34). The rending of this curtain from top to bottom, therefore, signifies God taking the initiative to break out of the confines of temple worship and priestly mediation, and to open up access to himself through the death of Jesus (see notes on Mark 11:12–26; cf. Hebrews 9:12–28; 10:19–20).

The second detail, which in certain respects is the key to Mark's entire Gospel, is the centurion's confession (v. 39). For it is only when the way of the cross has been concluded and the journey of discipleship undertaken to this point that Jesus' true identity and significance for salvation become apparent. Here, his convictions about the kingdom and his faith in God are exposed to the most extreme form of public scrutiny. And, in spite of all the ignominy and failure, rather than being found misguided and bankrupt, they disclose a quality of life and human being that can only have been formed and inspired by God. 'Truly this man was God's Son!'

6 Rumours of resurrection and the invitation to faith
Read Mark 16:1–8

Most English translations, including the NRSV, include what have become known as the 'shorter' and 'longer' endings of Mark. Most scholars believe that neither of these was original and that both were composed at a later stage (probably second century) to supply the ending either that Mark chose not to write or which was subsequently lost. Certainly, in comparison with the other Gospels, Mark's omission of resurrection narratives and conclusion with the irony that the women disciples who, having been entrusted with the good news, remain fearful and silent, seems strange. As we shall see, however, there are good reasons to maintain that this was the evangelist's intention.

The clue is to be found in the words of the young man (perhaps a heavenly messenger) to the women who, apparently, had come to anoint Jesus' body a considerable time after his death (decomposition would have been well under way given the climate) knowing that their access would be denied because of the large stone rolled against the entrance to the tomb (vv. 6–7). The angel supplies them with rumours of resurrection and an invitation, on behalf of Jesus, to meet with him once more in Galilee (cf. 14:28). This was to be communicated to the disciples and to Peter (mentioned by name because of his denial of Jesus).

But why Galilee? Many suggestions have been made, including that Galilee was the original locus for the resurrection encounters (cf. Matthew 28:16–20; John 21) and the place where Jesus as the Son of Man would return to bring the kingdom of God to fulfilment (cf. 8:38–9:1; 13:24–27). However, reflection upon Mark's presentation of Jesus commends another option. For Galilee was where Jesus' vocation and ministry took shape and where he called people to follow him in the way of the cross. Repeatedly, Mark stresses that the significance of Jesus for faith only becomes apparent as one undertakes the journey of discipleship with him. And at the completion of that journey not only is the glory of Jesus revealed through the Passion, but also the faith that informed his life and the vocation that inspired his ministry is entrusted to those who, having accompanied him throughout, must now embody that same faith and vocation. The return to Galilee, therefore, is the invitation to follow in Jesus' footsteps, to live out the good news of God, and so to discover that he continues to be the one who mediates God's presence and enables others to discover it for themselves.

This is Mark's genius. Rather than limiting the resurrection to the experience of a handful of people, he offers the invitation to share Jesus' faith to all prepared to follow him in the way of discipleship, an invitation that gains shape and definition through the pages of his Gospel.

GUIDELINES

The closing stages of Jesus' life as narrated by Mark have been both profound and uncomfortable. We have seen what people are capable of when feeling threatened or under pressure. We have discovered how revealing suffering can be and how, for perpetrator and victim alike, it possesses a transparent quality which discloses the inner self. We have also had to face up to the gulf that exists between beliefs and convictions entertained in the cloisters of the mind and those forged in the cauldron of human experience, where they must inform conduct, determine priorities and set the course our lives will take.

But, equally, we have confronted a vital truth about God which is communicated through Jesus' Passion and, in particular, his death and the words, 'My God, my God, why have you forsaken me?' For, in spite of first appearances and what we might want to believe, this whole episode is imbued with a profound holiness and divine quality. Not with a God who is out there and who is able to intervene to prevent this tragedy (cf. 'He saved others; he cannot save himself', 15:31); but with a God who informs the depth of human being encountered in Jesus. The cross is where we confront the God who is present as the absent one, to borrow a phrase from Dietrich Bonhoeffer, the God who has put his life and vision for humanity and all creation in our hands. Here on the cross, as throughout his life, Jesus radiates divine glory through his faith-filled, vision-inspired, Spirit-empowered example.

And what Jesus incarnated, each of us is invited to share. This is why there can be no final chapter to Mark's Gospel, just the promise that Jesus will be found wherever his faith is shared, his vision embraced and his ministry continued. For this is the substance of the risen life.

For further reading

Hugh Anderson, *The Gospel of Mark*, Marshall, Morgan & Scott, 1976

Ernest Best, *Mark: The Gospel as Story*, T. & T. Clark, 1983

Morna Hooker, *The Gospel According to Mark*, A. & C. Black, 1991

Ralph Martin, *Mark: Evangelist and Theologian*, Paternoster, 1972

Isaiah 40—55

Prophecy in full song

The steamy river plain was a contrast to the mountains of home. Here in southern Iraq, in mud-brick houses near a large canal, the exiled Jewish groups had been living for some fifty years. The banks of the waterway were dense with poplars, scrub and reeds, and mosquitoes added to the discomfort of the humid heat.

The Jewish communities maintained their identity under the leadership of the elders. Priests and prophets held to their own traditions and contributed to the care and guidance of the people. Crafts and businesses developed links with Babylonian society and sometimes became prosperous.

Meetings for worship were usually a time for grieving prayer. Anniversaries of the old disasters were occasions to confess sins and implore God's mercy, especially for the restoration of ruined Jerusalem and its temple. The meetings were held by the water's edge, but the feeling of ritual impurity in an alien land could not be banished, and the old joy of worship was laid aside.

Our story starts at one great gathering between 550 and 540 BC, about the time of the autumnal new year when in the old days hope and joy had sprung up in abundance. Now, the cantor could only keep to his plaintive theme, 'My way is hidden from the Lord, the Lord has forgotten me, the Lord has forsaken me.' The night was long, but as the light of morning broke, a prophet began to unfold an amazing message of salvation. In that extraordinary morning and on the succeeding days, he and others of his circle sang out again and again that the great turning point had come.

These glorious prophecies were subsequently written down, forming a cycle of song-like messages, the cycle we now have as chapters 40—55 in the great book of Isaiah. The question at once arises: why should it be found in this great tapestry of prophecy, subsumed under the name of the mighty prophet who had died a century before the exile?

The answer may well be that Isaiah had left disciples to preserve and continue his work in a chain of tradition capable of stretching through several generations. For this was the way of the East, as we see especially in the case of Arabian poets and Jewish rabbis. When the material contributed by Isaiah and his 'apostolic tradition' came to be handled and finalized by the scribes of later times, its cohesion as the product of the Isaiah chain was respected, and the whole kept together under Isaiah's name.

---

1   A way through the wilderness   *Read Isaiah 40:1–11*

For the ruined city and her children in exile there is wonderful news. The very first word cleaves the darkness, sounding twice: *na-amu na-amu*, 'Comfort, comfort!' It is a command in the plural, a word of God mediated by a prophet to a group, equipping them with a message for God's people and for Jerusalem. It seems to take us into the very dawn of the day of good tidings, the dawn when inspiration first stirs after a night of prayer and watching. In the meditating circle one prophet passes to the others an instruction from God, and it may be that some of the others in turn contribute in the fresh inspirations we shall meet in verses 3 and 6.

In this way, the prophets are instructed to console the people and the city, to speak to their sad heart with a kindness that restores life. The time of warfare and harsh service is completed, their sins atoned for, put away. They have suffered enough ('double' according to some translations—perhaps 'amply' is preferable).

In 40:3–5 another heavenly message is reported—a call to prepare through the wilderness the way of the Lord. Scenes of Jerusalem's former festivals underlie the vision. The ancient procession along the holy way, from the dry eastern hills, over the Mount of Olives and into the temple, signified the coming in of God as saviour of this land, city and people, but also as king of all creation. The call to clear and level this way carried a message of expectancy over the earth and through the heavens. All this lives again in the fresh prophetic inspiration, and carries a mighty meaning for the present life of the people. Beyond exile there opens the prospect of life in the light of God's presence, a world where the glory of the Lord is revealed.

In the old ceremonies, the incoming procession signified the victory of the Lord over Chaos. Runners, dancers, flocks of doves gave the news, the good tidings, ahead of the Lord. Now the prophets envisage again the proclamation of the good tidings to Zion and the other towns of Judah, and the Lord is pictured advancing with the spoils of war—

he has rescued his little ones and comes like a good shepherd, who would carry his tiny lambs and gently lead the ewes.

2 With wings like eagles *Read Isaiah 40:18–31*

The hope that flows from high moments of inspiration has to confront the despair and depression that gather around difficult circumstances. The prophetic ministry of comfort has to continue long to wrestle with a low-spirited, disbelieving, bitter people, who are hard to shift from their complaint that their way is hidden from the Lord, their right disregarded by their God (40:27).

Against such low spirits, the prophet spoke first of the infinite and incomparable power of the Lord. Here was a small community in the midst of a great foreign civilization, where foreign gods were exalted, and immense wealth and power flourished without reference to the God of Israel. Was he, then, really master of the world? The prophetic poetry depicts the Lord in his wisdom and might as Creator of all. Alone he made the universe, marking out and weighing as a craftsman might do on his table. In the light of his power, the mightiest nations are but a drop from a bucket, dust blown from the scales. Their gods are represented by images made by men, but the Lord, the true God, is beyond any imaginable likeness or dependency on human resource. Earth's great ones are but as grasshoppers beneath him. He has spread and fixed the heavens as the nomad raises and stretches out his goat-hair tent. Arrogant princes of the earth he can at any time bring down. Only look at the skies at night and think of the power and wisdom of him who knows and unfailingly musters every one of that bright host!

Yet more wonderful is his faithful kindness. So powerful and untiring as he is, he knows our frailty, and tenderly supports and renews those who 'wait' upon him—humble, trusting, watching in prayer. The bird usually translated 'eagle' (Hebrew *nesher*) may rather be the griffon vulture. With its eight-foot wingspan, it is a master at rising and floating high on currents of warm air. It provides an image of one who waits on the Lord and by his Spirit is brought mightily on his way.

3 I am He *Read Isaiah 41:1–4, 14–20*

To bring home to the weary people a vivid awareness of the Lord's unique and decisive reality, a great court scene is now imagined. The Lord calls to lands far across the seas, to peoples far and wide, to come for a judgment as to who or what is the supreme power of the universe. It is for each people to argue the case for the god they follow. But we have the impression of an awed silence, as the Lord upholds his own claim by unfolding a great work he is doing on the international stage. Beyond the northern limits of the Babylonian empire, the Persian conqueror Cyrus has been moving with amazing rapidity, taking power in state after state, from Persia to the Mediterranean. Who can have purposed and made possible these feats but the true God, who from the beginning to the end, through creation and history, is alone the Lord?

For the prophet's hearers the force of the argument is that here before them is the Lord's spokesman, able to give meaning to events on the world's stage, revealing a purpose of the Lord in it all which must soon spell the end of the Babylonian rule. Here indeed is evidence for them that the Lord is sovereign: 'I am the Lord from the first, and with the last I am He.' This pronoun 'He' has here a special ring of the one who is absolute, and unique, the one true God.

And from this mighty truth flows comfort for the Lord's followers: 'Fear not' (41:14). The people may have lamented in worship with words like Psalm 22:6, 'I am a worm and no man...' God's answer now is that this worm need not fear; soon it will turn and have power to demolish a mountain of difficulties.

Even though the Lord's people suffer at present like wanderers in a parched wilderness, soon the water of life will flow all about them. Their desert will become a place of trees like the garden of the Lord. They will have a 'redeemer' (go'el), a champion, one who stands by them in the worst situation. Moreover, he is 'the Holy One of Israel', the mysterious all-powerful God who loves them and never forsakes them.

4   Behold my Servant   *Read Isaiah 42:1–13*

Still drawing on the tradition of the former festivals, the prophetic inspiration creates more great scenes of a new beginning, a breaking through of the rays of the kingship of the Lord. Following the festal scenes of atonement and the Lord's processional entry already drawn upon, attention turns to the choice and empowering of the one who is to be God's chief agent, his royal Servant, the executive of his new reign.

The Lord speaks as though presenting his Servant to the festal assembly, itself representative of all creation: 'Behold my Servant...' He declares this beloved one to be chosen beyond all others, enabled by the gift of the Spirit to send out the rays of God's saving rule to all the world. The power given to this great mediator is most wonderfully shown in gentleness. Those whose spirit is almost broken, whose life is almost extinguished, he will tenderly nurture back to health.

Then the Lord addresses his Servant directly (vv. 5–7). The Creator's words create reality—his close partnership with his Servant, the power of that Servant (himself a 'covenant' or 'bond') to bind world society in good order and shed on it the light of true life (v. 6b), to free people from their fetters.

In the former festivals it would be a king of David's line on whom would be laid the ideal of mediating God's reign in the world. But for the present so much is not clearly stated. The scene is visionary and the person of the Servant is hidden in mystery. It is enough for the prophet's hearers to know that he is ready before God, his mission and success assured. The prophet has given a glimpse of God's wonderful new era before it springs forth (42:9).

The song-like prophecy passes easily into a fitting psalm for the new reign of God (42:10–12, resembling Psalms 96, 98, 149). For a while it seems the new era is all but here! With such songs the pre-exilic worshippers lived for a moment in a better world, the world yet to come. And now the exiles too are lifted to momentary experience of the kingdom of God, when all creatures of sea and land will unite in joyful praise of their Creator. ('Kedar' is an Arabian tribe, 'Sela' the Edomite capital. They represent the East, as 'the isles/coastlands' represent the West.)

At the end of our reading (42:13) is a glimpse of the might of God when he comes to war against the oppression and cruelty of this present age. Here is a champion whom no power will be able to withstand.

5   You are my witnesses   *Read Isaiah 43:8–21*

A scene like the one we met in chapter 41 is imagined. It is a great judicial assembly where the gods and their supporters are to put forward their claims to supremacy. Which can explain the upheavals of the present and of history? Which is therefore the guide of events, the shaper of all reality?

But only the Lord's claim is found worthy of mention. He asserts that he is the only saviour, the one who works and none can frustrate. He is the one true God, with none preceding him and none following (a contrast with foreign theologies which arranged their gods in a family sequence).

And the people of Israel, the Lord says, are his witnesses. The intimate bond he made with them is now to be the basis of a witness that will win faith from all peoples. Their experience of him as only saviour is to be shared with all nations.

But how poor are these witnesses! With good eyes and ears, they are yet unable to see and hear—unable to discern the work of God and respond to him with a full heart (43:8). But they were chosen precisely that they might know the Lord, believe, and live in and for his mighty reality (43:10).

Poor witnesses or not, they are about to be uplifted in a great salvation. As the Lord made a way of liberation for the slaves in Egypt through seas and deserts, overcoming Pharaoh's chariotry, so now he will make a way of salvation for the exiles in Babylonia. It can even be said, 'Think no more of the old salvation' (43:18)—a startling way of saying that an even greater liberation is approaching.

The way that is promised through the wilderness is like that in the prophecy of 40:3–5, a way where the Lord himself will go, heading for his temple as victor and saviour. But now the way appears as already itself an experience of the kingdom of God. The desert blossoms through the wondrous gift of water, and the wild animals gather peaceably to honour God. It is like the old vision of Isaiah (11:6–8), who knew that the peaceful love of all species, as depicted in the creation stories, was fundamental to the purpose of the Creator and must be fulfilled in the new kingdom of God.

6 You are my servant   *Read Isaiah 44:21–28*

How wonderful for those once called to the service of the Lord, but who have failed and sunk in shame, that they should hear again his voice, saying and repeating, 'You are my servant!' So it happens for the exiles, and God adds, 'I formed you; you will never be forgotten by me' (44:21). Already forgiven, already redeemed from sin and its captivity, they are simply told, 'Return to me' (44:22).

Already the prophet hears the hymns for God's new reign, and he takes up their summons to all creatures of heaven and earth—one great congregation—to sing the Creator's praise. They are to rejoice that the Lord has accomplished a central act in his work for all creation: redeeming the exiles, he has revealed his glory in Israel (44:23).

And now a specific message is addressed to the exiles (44:24–28). It is eloquently presented as a message from the divine Redeemer, the all-powerful Creator, whose prophets reveal truth beyond any knowledge of the famous Babylonian diviners and astrologers. God firmly purposes that the ruins of the Holy Land will be rebuilt, and that the Persian Cyrus will be his instrument in this, caring for the people as God's appointed shepherd. And this is a promise from the Creator who in the beginning had power to subdue the ocean of Chaos (44:27).

GUIDELINES

The prophecies we have read this week related to an important juncture in history. We were able to imagine their setting and force in southern Iraq five and a half centuries before the birth of Christ. But what can they mean to us in our era of television, air travel, nuclear power and computers?

As individuals and as a society we still know a sorrow of exile. In one way or another we may feel cut off from our mother country, the place of contentment where we deeply belonged, enjoyed esteem and served others without bitterness or fear. Though the gods of Babylon do not trouble us, our minds are no less affected by the idols made by human hands and uplifted in ruthless greed.

Shall we too not be glad of a prophet who tells us of a saviour near at hand, and a dawning kingdom of joy in which we can have part? Yes, we may read again and again his thrilling words, and take to ourselves his gospel of forgiveness, his vision of the one true God, infinite and invincible, who has never ceased to love us. Our spirits lost the power to see and hear the truth, yet still he reckoned us his servants and his witnesses, still he called us to come to him, bought back from enslavement, redeemed. The message still rings out that he is ready to lead us home, and that the long way through the desert at his side will already be an experience of beauty, love and peace.

20–26 APRIL   **ISAIAH 45:1—51:11**

1   The treasures of darkness   *Isaiah 45:1–8, 22–25*

Keeping religion and politics separate would have made little sense to the Israelites, the Babylonians, or any other ancient people. The king of Babylon, Nabonidus from northern Iraq, was losing support because of his promotion of his god Sin at the expense of Marduk of Babylon, 'king of the gods'. Cyrus the Persian, as he conquered the empires of the Medes and of the Lydians, reigning now from Iran to the edge of Europe, was ready to present himself to the Babylonians as champion of their god.

No wonder that soon the great Babylonian empire fell easily into his hands (539BC), and he entered Babylon peacefully as the ruler that Marduk had searched out from all countries and named as his righteous minister over all the world. Cyrus at once befriended the captives in Babylon, allowing them to return home and encouraging them to restore their places of worship. This new policy applied also to the Jewish exiles, for whom the way was now open to return and restore the Lord's house in Jerusalem.

Some time before Cyrus conquered Babylonia, the Isaiah prophets were already giving a bold interpretation of his progress. Having already spoken of him with cautious veiling as 'the one from the East' (41:2), they now name him (44:28; 45:1). Having designated Cyrus 'my Shepherd' (44:28), the Lord goes further and calls him 'my Anointed' (45:1). Just as Nebuchadnezzar king of Babylon had once been called the Lord's Servant (Jeremiah 27:6), so Cyrus is now seen as chosen and empowered by the Lord to rule the nations. Amazing victories will be given him by God, as also the vaults of treasure hoarded by the fallen empires. His titles of honour will be given him by the Lord, even though Cyrus does not clearly know the one true God as the Lord, the Holy One of Israel.

So do many things happen on the world stage, guided and given by the God who is not recognized. At every turn God is there, though his footprints are not seen (Psalm 77:19). There are no politics without him—shaping, judging, throwing down, building up.

And what of the treasures of darkness (45:3)? The poetry goes deeper than the particular reference. To each whom God calls it brings a promise, that doors will be opened, bars broken down, and wonderful treasures bestowed in the place of darkness.

The prophet's view of the divine salvation moves to and fro between Israel and the entire world. Cyrus is to rule the world 'for the sake of my servant Jacob' (45:4), but there is also a call for all the ends of the earth 'to turn to me and be saved' (45:22). Most solemnly the Lord has pledged, and will never go back, that every knee shall bow to him—all become his worshippers. All will know him as the only source of reality (45:7), and in him the offspring of Israel will find true glory (45:23–25).

2 I will carry and I will save *Read Isaiah 46*

Just as the Isaiah prophets foresee the victorious procession of the Lord to his temple (40:3–11; 52:7–12), so they foresee a procession of shame for the defeated gods of Babylon, taken from their temples into exile (46:1–2). 'Bel' is Marduk 'king of the gods', while 'Nebo' is the son of Marduk and the god of wisdom and writing. Aptly represented by their images, which are taken down and loaded on to pack animals, they are helpless. As we noted in our previous reading, events turned out rather differently when Cyrus actually took over Babylon. But our prophets, ahead of the event, are concerned to represent graphically the essential truth of the unique power of the Lord and his imminent salvation.

The idea of helpless gods that need to be carried is developed further. The images have to be lifted, then they stand where they are put, fitly representing gods unable to answer or save. By contrast the Lord is one who himself carries—with love and might he carries his own. And his care is not just for early years but all through life. It is an assurance for young and old: 'I will carry and I will save.'

The 'bird of prey from the East... the man of my counsel' (46:11) is the Persian conqueror Cyrus. The thought of a great bird's flight gives a fitting picture of the amazing swiftness of his progress. Our prophet sees deeply into the political upheavals of his day and recognizes the work of the Lord, set to keep his promise of salvation: 'I have spoken and I will bring it to pass.' Most marvellous of all, not even the transgressions and stubbornness of those he means to save will turn aside his purpose (46:8–12).

3 Water from the rock *Read Isaiah 48:9–22*

Mingling with themes already announced are now some words in a rather severe tone. Coming at the end of the first half of our cycle of prophecies, this chapter seems to reflect the difficulty of the preacher's task. Even with a thrilling gospel to proclaim, the prophets have met with a disappointing response—negative, mean-minded. They therefore have some sharp things to say, before the glorious message takes wing again in the second half of the cycle (chapters 49—55).

Earlier in the exile, Ezekiel had stressed that God would save his people not for their own merit, but for the sake of his name (Ezekiel 36:22–32). This point is now repeated. The people have not deserved that his annihilating judgment be held back, but something deep in his nature and in his purpose for creation has worked for their forgiveness and salvation. It is on this basis that the Lord is guiding a turn of history through Cyrus. In all the changes God is present; and he gives clear guidance, sending his prophet and his Spirit.

At the former festivals there would be glad music of song, timbrel, lyre and harp to acclaim the coming of the Lord, then silence to hear what he would pronounce through his prophet. And sometimes he might remind them of his commandments and add, 'Oh that you would hearken to me... I would feed you with the finest wheat and satisfy you with honey from the rock.' All this we can see from Psalm 81. Our prophets draw on that old scene as they give the Lord's present word: 'Oh that you would hearken to my commandments! Then your peace would be like a river, and your righteousness like the waves of the sea!'

The 'peace' and 'righteousness' here mean the bounty of God, the gifts of life which he longs to bestow, deep and broad as the ocean. And the chapter ends with promise of abundant salvation and a marvellous exodus from Babylon, but also including a final cautionary note.

4   A light to the nations   *Read Isaiah 49:1–16*

The second part of our cycle of prophecy begins here and does indeed take new wings of visionary power. We have already seen (in chapter 42) how, in visions of the new reign of God, there would come a scene of anointing for one who is to be the agent, the channel, the 'Servant' of the reign. In the vision of chapter 42 the commission was clearly given, the purpose of God was established, but the person of the Servant was hidden in mystery.

And so it is still, even as the prophet brings us the Servant's voice. The identity is still not disclosed, but the intense vision of the seer attains to wonderful insights into the work of the chosen one. The streams that quicken this dramatic vision flow from several springs— from deep wisdom of ancient royal ceremonies, from the bitter lessons of royal history, and from the hardships common to the servants of God.

Our prophet first carries the voice of the Servant struggling with failure, then the voice of the Lord making a wonderful reply. The Servant's speech is to the whole world. In kingly style he tells how God prepared him for his role even before he was born, how he made him like a divine weapon, concealed till the right moment, how he had pronounced to him the formula of ordination, 'You are my Servant', and given him the title 'Israel'. This title means 'God reigns' and indicates one who will serve God's glory and have the role of 'father of the nation' to seek and to bring home the nation of Israel (49:5–6).

But the Servant has more to tell. He describes how he took up his work and came to feel that it was all a failure, yet still held on to trust in God. He relates how God has answered him and declared that the task which seemed too heavy is in fact too light; his Servant is not only to raise up and bring to God the tribes of Israel, but also to be a light to the nations, bringing them the salvation of the kingdom of God.

Our prophet now carries the voice of God directly (49:7–12), addressing his Servant with strengthening words for all he is destined to do. Yes, his way is through tribulation, scorned by the great of the world. But in the end kings will fall down before him. In victory he will bind his people anew under God and lead the captives to freedom. (In 49:12 'Syene/Sinim' denotes Asswan, in the remote south of the Egyptian realm.)

A short hymn of joy at this prospect (49:13) is followed by a most precious passage (49:14–16). In lamenting worship, ruined Jerusalem and her children have complained that the Lord has forgotten his once beloved sanctuary-city. The prophet gives the Lord's resounding answer. When a mother can become indifferent to her baby—almost inconceivable—the Lord will still be loving and watching over his dear one. How could he forget her? Her form is engraved on the palm of his hands; his plan for her rebuilding is ever in his heart.

5 Braving shame and spitting *Read Isaiah 50:1–11*

We hear again an echo of the reproaches raised against the Lord in the services of lamentation. Why has he 'sent away', that is 'divorced', his 'wife' Zion? Or why has he 'sold' her children into slavery? The Lord's reply (50:1) is that though estrangement did occur, and the children were handed over to bondage, all because of grave sin, yet there was no final transaction. The Lord is not bound by any deed of divorce or shackled by debt! The way is open for the restoration of Zion and her children.

The prophet sees the Lord arguing his case with such compelling power that none will come forward with further complaint (50:2). Has he lost his old strength for salvation, God asks? Is he not still the mighty Creator with sovereign power over seas and skies (50:2–3)?

And now the prophet brings us again the voice of the one appointed to be the Lord's chief Servant in his coming kingdom (50:4–9). Even more than in chapter 49, there is expression of the profound insight that this royal service must take the way of suffering. In the prophet's vision, the Servant therefore declares to the world that the Lord inspires him with strengthening words, leads him into an obedience which braves persecution, shame and spitting, and finally gives him victory over his adversaries. Happy those who fear the Lord and obey this his Servant, for though his way must go through deep darkness, in the end it will be his foes who suffer in the fires of the hatred they have kindled (v. 11).

There is an interesting glimpse of the prophetic life in verse 4. 'Those who are taught' (*limmudim*, as also in 8:16), can be understood as the prophetic disciples. Before dawn they sit together in meditation, and at first light the Lord may stir a word in the ear of one of them. The revelation is shared and then taken to the people to encourage the weary. This prophetic life demands self-sacrifice, and it makes a good comparison for the sacrificial work of the royal Servant of the Lord.

6 Awake, O arm of the Lord! *Read Isaiah 51:1–11*

Even for the devout, who earnestly seek after the Lord and his righteousness, it is hard to have confident hope. They seem so few and powerless, the worldly forces so strong. But the prophet bids them consider Abraham and Sarah and the number of their descendants—so the blessing of God can make the few into many. The dismal ruins of Jerusalem, likewise, he can make into his own garden, the well of life.

The Lord indeed affirms that his law will go forth—his new reign shining out from his throne-centre in Zion, a light of healing and justice for all peoples. With an amazing emphasis on the enduring nature of his salvation, he sees the great structure of the universe by comparison as transitory, like dispersing smoke or a worn-out garment. So the devout must not fear human cruelty. Already his kingdom is come in their hearts (51:7), the beginning of a salvation which shall be for ever.

The inspired prophet lends himself to be the very instrument of God's awakening power. He will soon be calling Jerusalem out of the deep sleep of death (51:17). But first he cries 'Awake, awake' to 'the arm of the Lord', reminding that mighty arm of its conquest of Chaos (symbolized as a dragon and the monster Rahab) in the beginning of time. Once again we see our prophets drawing from reservoirs of tradition, releasing new poetic power from customs and words of ancient worship. The style of invoking God to action is found in lamenting psalms (e.g. Psalm 44:23, 26), but here the context is all radiant confidence and joy. The ransomed of the Lord are pictured streaming into Zion as happy festal pilgrims, while angels of joy chase away the spirits of sorrow and sighing.

GUIDELINES

From the sixth century BC have wonderfully come down to us the glowing words that have been our portion this week. Can these messages to the ancient exiles still bear fruit in our times? Surely, as we wait humbly before our Lord with these sayings, he will for us also begin to open doors, break down barriers, and bring us the treasures of darkness, hoards from the secret places. To diminished communities of his Church he will declare his power to make the few many, the desolate place once again his garden, with its fountain of life. He will show us the salvation which endures when heaven and earth crumble, the deliverance which comes to us not for our merits, but for the fulfilment of his love.

And as we continue to ponder that ancient poetry, he will assure us of his reign, which is to rise like the sun over all his creatures, but which already may shine in our hearts. He will assure us of that great homecoming, when the ransomed of the Lord at last enter his house with songs of joy. But also he will strengthen us to keep bravely with the one who mediates his reign, and has first to suffer before entering into glory. Through a deeper darkness this royal Servant has taken his way, and from it brings us treasures beyond all price.

O Jesus, who for our sake
did not hide your face from shame and spitting,
help us to take the way of reverence and obedience,
and in times of darkness to see your light
and ever trust
in the Father, the Son and Holy Spirit.

148

1   **How beautiful on the mountains**   *Read Isaiah 52:7–15*

When we were reading 40:3–11 we noted that underlying the vision of
the Lord's procession into Zion was the memory of the chief procession
in the old Israelite festivals, a sacrament of the Lord's new reign. This is
all the clearer as the vision is renewed. Just as the people had watched
from Zion's walls, seeing first the runners with tidings of salvation coming over the Mount of Olives, then the holy procession itself descending into full view, so a newly revived Jerusalem will watch for and see
the messengers and procession of God her king. How beautiful will
seem the feet of the runner who is first to breast the hill and shout the
good news of victory and *shalom*! How carefully those of the sacred
orders who carry the sacred vessels will have purified themselves after
long years of exile, for the Lord himself is present in the column, and
his aura envelops and protects it before and behind!

The prophets have thus seen the holy kingdom drawing near. And
now the scene changes and their soul is filled with revelation concerning the Lord's chief Servant, the one who is called to execute the wishes of the heavenly king. First they hear the Lord's voice pronouncing
the destiny, assuring the triumph of his Servant (52:13–15). The throne
of victory shall indeed be his (v. 13).

In verse 14 most translators find a reference already to his sufferings
(e.g. RSV 'His appearance was so marred'). A slightly different spelling
in the great scroll of Isaiah found among the Dead Sea Scrolls suggests
a much smoother translation (with a phrase found in Psalm 45:7):

As many were dumbfounded at (him),
So I have anointed his face above men
And his form above mankind.

In verse 15 where some translators put 'startle' (RSV), it is better to
follow the old rendering 'sprinkle/purify'—an act of royal and priestly
authority:

So shall he purify many nations,
while kings shut their mouths before him,
for things never told they see
and things unheard of they contemplate.

Thus the oracle of the Lord has first established the supremacy of his Servant, high over all the kings of the world. It is like an Old Testament 'transfiguration', a glimpse of the final glory before the story of humiliation begins.

2   Bearing the sin of many   *Read Isaiah 53:1–12*

'Who could believe our revelation?' So begins this most awesome chapter. The prophets, chanting together and with repetitions as in a chorus, are to describe a shocking enigma, and then give the amazing explanation that has been disclosed to them by God.

Following hard on the oracle of God about his Servant (52:13–15), their story about an unnamed figure who grew up before the Lord without appearance of majesty is clearly the story of this Servant, yet there is an air of mystery as the designation is held back till verse 11. There are still pointers to his royal person—the imagery of the tree shoot (53:2) and the shepherd (implied, 53:6), the mediation of the Lord's rule through the Servant's hand (53:10), the promise of conquest and spoil (53:12). But contrary to expectations, he appears as one deprived of his rightful majesty, loaded with sufferings, and consequently shunned, scorned as one thought to be deservedly smitten by God.

But (from v. 4) the 'arm of the Lord', the mighty divine work, begins to be uncovered. The prophets reveal that the Servant was suffering not for his own, but for 'our' sins, the transgressions of the 'many', the iniquity of all. The sheep had gone astray, and the shepherd was ready to die for them. Quiet and uncomplaining was the Servant when oppressed. No violence, no deceit was found in him. He was truly God's righteous one. He had offered himself as a sacrifice to make the multitudes right with God. Upon himself he took the load of their sins. His wounds were healing for them; his death was life for them. Such humility, such willing service of God, such love! This self-sacrifice became the mightiest divine work, the door of God's new kingdom.

The triumph is set out from verse 10b (my own translation):

Truly his soul has made an offering for sin.
So he shall see descendants, for he shall live long,
And in his hand the will of the Lord shall prosper.

The outcome of his soul's pain he shall see
and be satisfied.

By his knowledge (of me) the Righteous One makes right,
yes, multitudes he makes right,
for he has borne their guilt.

Therefore I give him the multitudes as his share,
and he may take the many as his spoil,
in reward for baring his soul to death
and being numbered with sinners,
though it was the sin of the multitudes that he carried,
and he was interposing himself for sinners.

Thus the vision of the service whereby the kingdom comes! In their time the prophets will have been looking for some fulfilment of the ideal laid upon the house of David. But so deep have they seen, that no time or place or person could here be fittingly named. Deeper than time itself they have seen, and deeper than the logic of legal justice. They have seen the Lamb slain from the foundation of the world. They have seen Calvary and its fruits.

3 Break forth into singing   *Read Isaiah 54:1–8*

An outburst of song was not a matter of stiff-standing bespectacled perusal of a music book, but of swaying and clapping and dancing feet. It was like swimming in waves of joy, a yielding of oneself to the tide of God's goodness.

After the prophecies of the Lord's way to Zion and the redeeming of sinners through his Servant's sacrifice, the continuation is wonderfully right. Desolate Zion is called to just such a joyful celebration: 'Sing, O barren one, break forth into singing!' With shifting metaphors the holy city is pictured as an Eastern woman grieving and ashamed of her child-lessness. Whether as barren, or forsaken, or widowed, she has had to bear sorrow and reproach. But now she is to have a marvellous family and husband, and will be as it were the envy of all the women who scorned her. She is pictured as a Bedouin woman who zestfully extends her tent for her growing family.

Zion's husband is none other than the Lord. She is bride and queen, while he is husband and king. Yes, there was an estrangement—'For a brief moment I forsook you, but with great compassion now I gather you.' His love for her is everlasting. He is her redeemer, the one closest to her and faithful to deliver her from trouble.

These traditional pictures and metaphors express an astounding intimacy and involvement of God with his people, the dedicated people that he means to be the heart of his universe. As our own hymns about Zion readily show, it was a faith, a teaching, an experience, that carried through into the Church. Here also we are to see the Beloved of our Lord, beautiful through his everlasting love, with a growing family and songs of joy for his redeeming work.

4   My covenant of peace   *Read Isaiah 54:9–17*

The winter rain in Palestine often comes heavily and continues for two or three days. All the more striking then, when the sun reappears and a rainbow is set against the receding darkness of the sky.

This beautiful bow, curved across the world, was to the Hebrews a sign of the everlasting covenant between God and every living creature upon the whole earth, the sign explained at the conclusion of the story of Noah and the flood (Genesis 9:8–17). This covenant was God's promise that he would never again release the flood to destroy all creatures. Two features are prominent: it is *universal*, a covenant which God has made for all animals as well as mankind, and it is *everlasting*, never to be rescinded.

Like this covenant given in the days of Noah, according to our reading today, is the covenant of peace which God now gives in the time of Zion's restoration. The universal aspect remains latent in this utterance, and the emphasis falls on the enduring character ('Though the mountains depart, my love will never leave you...'). It is a promise directed to Zion (for the Hebrew has 'you' in the feminine singular) and she is further addressed as 'one afflicted, storm-tossed, not comforted'. The holy city is to be adorned with precious stones, like a bejewelled bride. Her people will have great *shalom*, abundance of all that is good, and will be the 'taught' (*limmudim*) of the Lord. This word, which we met in 50:4, can mean 'disciples' and would here indicate a total commitment in mission, a life centred on the love and service of the Lord.

The promise to Zion concludes with reiteration that the Lord will not again send armies against her. In disputes her tongue will prevail. The restored Jerusalem was indeed to survive many centuries, but at last was destroyed by Roman armies in AD70. The truth of the prophet's message must lie deeper than the surface of history. He saw through to the unshakeable, invincible purpose of God for his people. 'Zion' in the end is the symbol of the heart of his creation, not an earthly city; she

SUBSCRIPTIONS

NEW DAYLIGHT—GUIDELINES—LIVEWIRES

Please note our new subscription rates for 1998–1999. From **1 May 1998** the new subscription rates will be:

Individual subscriptions covering 3 issues for under 5 copies, payable in advance (including postage and packing):

		UK	surface	airmail
LIVEWIRES (8–10 yr olds)	3 volumes p.a.	£12.00	£13.50	£15.00
GUIDELINES	each set of 3 p.a.	£9.60	£10.80	£13.20
NEW DAYLIGHT	each set of 3 p.a.	£9.60	£10.80	£13.20
NEW DAYLIGHT LARGE PRINT	each set of 3 p.a.	£15.00	£18.60	£21.00

Group Subscriptions covering 3 issues for 5 copies or more, sent to ONE address (post free):

LIVEWIRES	£10.50	3 volumes p.a.
GUIDELINES	£8.10	each set of 3 p.a.
NEW DAYLIGHT	£8.10	each set of 3 p.a.
NEW DAYLIGHT LARGE PRINT	£13.50	each set of 3 p.a.

Please note that the annual billing period for Group Subscriptions runs from 1 May to 30 April.

Copies of the notes may also be obtained from Christian bookshops:

LIVEWIRES	£3.50 each copy
GUIDELINES and NEW DAYLIGHT	£2.70 each copy
NEW DAYLIGHT LARGE PRINT	£4.50 each copy

Please note that the Lightning Bolts range also includes volumes of undated daily Bible reading notes for 10–14 year olds. Contact your local bookshop or BRF direct for details.

SUBSCRIPTIONS

❏ I would like to give a gift subscription (please complete both name and address sections below)
❏ I would like to take out a subscription myself (complete name and address details only once)
❏ Please send me details of 3-year subscriptions

This completed coupon should be sent with appropriate payment to BRF. Alternatively, please write to us quoting your name, address, the subscription you would like for either yourself or a friend (with their name and address), the start date and credit card number, expiry date and signature if paying by credit card.

Gift subscription name _____

Gift subscription address _____

_____ Postcode _____

Please send to the above, beginning with the May 1998 issue:

(please tick box)	UK	SURFACE	AIR MAIL
LIVEWIRES	❏ £12.00	❏ £13.50	❏ £15.00
GUIDELINES	❏ £9.60	❏ £10.80	❏ £13.20
NEW DAYLIGHT	❏ £9.60	❏ £10.80	❏ £13.20
NEW DAYLIGHT LARGE PRINT	❏ £15.00	❏ £18.60	❏ £21.00

Please complete the payment details below and send your coupon, with appropriate payment to: **The Bible Reading Fellowship, Peter's Way, Sandy Lane West, Oxford OX4 5HG**

Your name _____

Your address _____

_____ Postcode _____

Total enclosed £ _____ (cheques should be made payable to 'BRF')

Payment by cheque ❏ postal order ❏ Visa ❏ Mastercard ❏ Switch ❏

Card number: [ ][ ][ ][ ] [ ][ ][ ][ ] [ ][ ][ ][ ] [ ][ ][ ][ ]

Expiry date of card: [ ][ ][ ][ ]   Issue number (Switch): [ ][ ][ ][ ]

Signature (essential if paying by credit/Switch card) _____

NB: BRF notes are also available from your local Christian bookshop.

GL0198   The Bible Reading Fellowship is a Registered Charity

BRF PUBLICATIONS ORDER FORM

Please ensure that you complete and send off both sides of this order form.

Please send me the following book(s):

		Quantity	Price	Total
3556	Reflecting the Glory (T. Wright)	_____	£6.99	_____
3548	The Way In New Testament, pbk (D. Winter)	_____	£6.99	_____
3253	The Matthew Passion (J. Fenton)	_____	£5.99	_____
3509	The Jesus Prayer (S. Barrington-Ward)	_____	£3.50	_____
3295	Livewires: Footsteps and Fingerprints (R. Sharples)	_____	£3.50	_____
3296	Livewires: Families and Feelings (H. Butler)	_____	£3.50	_____
3522	Livewires: Friends and Followers (S. Herbert)	_____	£3.50	_____
3523	Livewires: Tiptoes and Fingertips (B. Ogden)	_____	£3.50	_____
3549	Livewires: Trackers and Trainers (R. Sharples)	_____	£3.50	_____
3550	Livewires: Searchlights and Secrets (J. Hyson)	_____	£3.50	_____
2821	People's Bible Commentary: Genesis (H. Wansbrough)	_____	£5.99	_____
2824	People's Bible Commentary: Mark (R.T. France)	_____	£7.99	_____
3280	People's Bible Commentary: 1 Corinthians (J. Murphy-O'Connor)	_____	£7.99	_____
3281	People's Bible Commentary: Galatians (J. Fenton)	_____	£4.99	_____
3297	People's Bible Commentary: Revelation (M. Maxwell)	_____	£7.99	_____
3250	Prophets and Poets (ed. G. Emmerson)	_____	£8.99	_____

Total cost of books £ _____

Postage and packing (see over) £ _____

TOTAL £ _____

See over for payment details. All prices are correct at time of going to press, are subject to the prevailing rate of VAT and may be subject to change without prior warning.

NB: All BRF titles are also available from your local Christian bookshop.

GL0198   The Bible Reading Fellowship is a Registered Charity

PAYMENT DETAILS

Please complete the payment details below and send with appropriate payment and completed order form to:

The Bible Reading Fellowship,
Peter's Way,
Sandy Lane West,
Oxford OX4 5HG

Name _____

Address _____

_____

_____ Postcode _____

Total enclosed £ _____ (cheques should be made payable to 'BRF')

Payment by cheque ❏ postal order ❏ Visa ❏ Mastercard ❏ Switch ❏

Card number: ▢▢▢▢ ▢▢▢▢ ▢▢▢▢ ▢▢▢▢

Expiry date of card: ▢▢▢▢   Issue number (Switch): ▢▢▢▢

Signature (essential if paying by credit/Switch card) _____

POSTAGE AND PACKING CHARGES				
order value	UK	Europe	Surface	Air Mail
£6.00 & under	£1.25	£2.25	£2.25	£3.50
£6.01–£14.99	£3.00	£3.50	£4.50	£6.50
£15.00–£29.99	£4.00	£5.50	£7.50	£11.00
£30.00 & over	free	prices on request		

Alternatively you may wish to order books using the BRF telephone order hotline:
01865 748227